Second Edition

Mass Communication Law in Rhode Island

Linda Lotridge Levin

NEW FORUMS

Stillwater, Oklahoma
U.S.A.

This book may be ordered in bulk quantities at discount
from New Forums Press, Inc., P.O. Box 876, Stillwater,
OK 74076
[Federal I.D. No. 73-11232391]

ISBN 10: 1-58107-007-1

Table of Contents

About the Author

Linda Lotridge Levin is an Associate Professor of Journalism at The University of Rhode Island, Kingston, Rhode Island, where her courses include mass media law. She holds a BA in journalism from Michigan State University and an MS in journalism from Boston University. She is a former reporter and editor for *The Providence Journal* and a freelance writer and columnist whose specialties have included medicine, American history and law. Her most recent book is *To Understand: The history of a 10-year dialogue between New England and Soviet editors*, published in 1993 by *The Boston Globe*.

About the Rhode Island Press Association

The Rhode Island Press Association traces its origins to 1886. Today it is a non-profit, educational association which promotes the welfare of the newspaper industry in the state and encourages high standards of conduct and professional ethics in the practice of journalism. It represents most of the daily, weekly and twice weekly newspapers in the state. The association sponsors an annual newspaper contest, awards an annual scholarship to a college journalism student, and sponsors seminars for high school and college students interested in journalism as well as seminars and workshops for practicing journalists. In addition, it operates the Rhode Island Journalism Hall of Fame. The association's headquarters and the hall of fame are in the Department of Journalism at the University of Rhode Island in Kingston, R.I. The telephone number is 401-792-4287.

Preface

This text was written to provide journalists and students of media law with an overview of the laws and regulations relating to the media in Rhode Island.

Anyone who wants more in depth information about a particular case or law can refer to the appropriate citation in the endnotes and go to the original, written source, such as the opinion of a particular court or the state statute.

Court opinions from the Rhode Island Supreme Court can be found in the *Atlantic Reporter* (A. or A.2d). Court opinions from the federal system are cited using either F. Supp. (*Federal Supplement* for the district court) or F. or F.2d (*Federal Reporter* for the appeals court). The number preceding the title of the reporter refers to the volume; the number following is the page on which the opinion begins. The date at the end of the case citation is the year the court decided the case.

State statutes also are cited in the endnotes. For instance, the Open Meetings Law is R.I. Gen. Laws 42 46 1. The numbers indicate, in sequence, the chapter, the article, and the section of the law.

All of the volumes cited in this book are available at the State Law Library in the Licht Judicial Complex on Benefit Street in Providence and in some college and university libraries in the state.

The opinions of the attorney general (Op. Atty. Gen.) are cited in the chapter on open meetings. These opinions are non binding advisories and are available in the Civil Division of the Office of the Attorney General.

I would like to thank Professor Mel Topf of Roger Williams University, and Leonard I. Levin, my husband and the metro editor of *The Providence Journal*, for reading the manuscript for this book and giving me valuable guidance. I also thank Christopher Beall, a *Providence Journal* reporter, who shared his research into the opinions of the attorney general.

> *Linda Lotridge Levin*
> The University of Rhode Island

The Courts in Rhode Island

Rhode Island has a unified state court system comprising four statewide courts.

The Rhode Island Supreme Court is the state's final appellate court. It considers appeals in criminal and civil cases and renders advisory opinions to the executive and legislative branches of government regarding the constitutionality of legislation. The Supreme Court also supervises state trial courts.

The Superior Court serves as the state's trial court with the sole jurisdiction to try all felony cases. The court also hears civil cases in which damages of $10,000 or more are being sought. It has concurrent jurisdiction with the District Court when the damages sought are between $5,000 and $10,000. The Superior Court hears equity cases. It hears appeals from the district court on civil and criminal cases and appeals of local probate and municipal court decisions.

The District Court hears criminal misdemeanor cases, if the defendant waives the right to a jury trial. It also presides over civil trials in which total damages sought are $5,000 or less, or if all parties agree to a $10,000 maximum. The court has jurisdiction over cases in which people are hospitalized involuntarily, and it hears appeals of decisions rendered by the state tax administrator.

The Family Court hears and decides divorce cases, including child support and custody, and matters relating to delinquent, truant, abused or mentally disabled children. It also handles adoption and paternity proceedings.

The U.S. District Court is the federal court in Rhode Island. It decides questions of law that arise under the U.S. Con-

1

stitution. Trials of civil and criminal cases brought under federal law are held in this court, and disputes involving state laws or citizens of different states are settled in the federal court. Appeals from this court go before the federal Circuit Court of Appeals in Boston.

Media Rights in Rhode Island: The First Amendment and Parallel State Statute

The First Amendment to the U.S. Constitution states:

> Congress shall make no law respecting an establishment of religion, or prohibiting the free exercise thereof; or abridging the freedom of speech, or of the press; or the right of the people peaceably to assemble, and to petition the Government for a redress of grievances.

Article I, Section 20, of the Constitution of the State of Rhode Island and Providence Plantations* states:

> The liberty of the press being essential to the security of freedom in a state, any person may publish sentiments on any subject, being responsible for the abuse of that liberty; and in all trials for libel, both civil and criminal, the truth, unless published from malicious motives, shall be sufficient defense to the person charged. (This remains unchanged from 1843 Rhode Island Constitution.)

In addition, Article I, Section 21, states:

> The citizens have a right in a peaceable manner to assemble for their common good, and to apply to those invested with the powers of government, for redress of grievances, or for

* Henceforth, the name of the state will appear as Rhode Island.

other purposes by petition, address, or remonstrance. No law abridging the freedom of speech shall be enacted. (This last sentence was added when the state constitution was modernized and amended in 1986.)

Defamation in Rhode Island

Defamation is the injuring of the good name or reputation by tending to damage the person's standing in the community. Defamation can take the form of either libel (written or broadcast) or slander (spoken).

Rhode Island has no statute defining defamation; rather, the definition used in its courts today derives from common law and previous courts' decisions.

That definition dates to 1825 when the Federal Circuit Court of Appeals in Rhode Island ruled that writings, printings, and caricatures tending to expose persons to public hatred, contempt, ridicule, aversion or disgrace were libelous. (1)

In 1897, the Rhode Island Supreme Court broadened its earlier definition, saying, "We think it may be safely said that any words, if false and malicious, imputing conduct which injuriously affects a man's reputation, or which tends to degrade him in society, or bring him into public hatred and contempt, are in their nature defamatory.... (2) In 1985, the state's high court reaffirmed that definition. (3)

The state Supreme Court also has ruled that there is no distinction between broadcast and print defamation. (4) Quoting from federal rulings, the court said, it is "clear that broadcasting of defamatory matter by means of radio or television is libel, whether or not it is read from a manuscript," and thus the "broadcaster (is placed) upon the same footing as the publisher of a newspaper." (5)

In addition to common law, Rhode Island has state statutes which cover some aspects of defamation, such as truth as a defense to libel and slander (6) and libel of a deceased person. (7) They will be discussed in this chapter.

Basic Considerations

For libel to occur, the following elements must be present:
- Publication to a third party
- Identification of the plaintiff (i.e., the person who alleges the defamation)
- Defamatory words
- Fault (ie., the defamation was published as a result of negligence or recklessness)

The Rhode Island Supreme Court outlined these elements in 1989 in Healey v. New England Newspapers, Inc. The court said that in a defamation action, a plaintiff must prove "(a) a false and defamatory statement concerning another; (b) an unprivileged publication to a third party; (c) fault amounting at least to negligence on the part of the publisher; and (d) damages, unless the statement is actionable irrespective of special harm." (8)

Publication

To win a court case, a libel plaintiff must prove that a defamatory statement was communicated to a person other than the alleged defamed person. For libel, this means that newspapers publish when they circulate even a single copy of an issue, and radio and television stations publish when they air a broadcast. When dealing with newspapers and broadcasting, it is not difficult to prove publication or communication to a third person. Libel also can be published in press releases, business letters, and office memos.

Communication of spoken words—slander—was defined

---

* "Actual mailice" is defined later in this chapter in the section titled Fault: Defining the Alleged Defamed Person.

by the Rhode Island Supreme Court in a 1965 case, Gaudette v. Carter. The court stated that "unless defamatory words are communicated to a third person and understood by him, there can be no recovery in an action for damages for slander." (9)

The state Supreme Court has said that an essential element of libel is that the defamatory publication should be by printing or writing or by signs. (10) As noted, the court has equated broadcast and print libel. (11)

Three recent cases have dealt with republication or reprinting of allegedly defamatory information. Martin v. Wilson Publishing Co., (12) a 1985 case, involved the republication of rumors. At issue was whether it was permissible for the defendant newspaper to publish false defamatory rumors (even about a public figure) when the newspapers believed the substance of the rumors to be untrue.

In Martin v. Wilson, the state Supreme Court, citing earlier rulings, (13) said that "one who republishes libelous or slanderous material is subject to liability just as if he had published it originally." (14) The court went on to say:

> Republication of false, defamatory statements about an individual may be printed only in extremely limited situations in which the republication accurately attributes such statements to an identified and responsible source, and thus publication of false or baseless rumors makes the publisher responsible under the 'actual malice'* test of the United States Supreme Court's *New York Times* decision for ascertaining the truth of the underlying defamatory material in such circumstances.(15)

The second case, Healey v. New England Newspapers, Inc., (16) was a complicated libel case brought by a local physician who, a newspaper article claimed, had failed to aid a heart attack victim.

In ruling against the newspaper, *The Pawtucket Evening Times*, the state's Supreme Court chastised the reporter for including opinions critical of the physician without including information that probably would have cleared him. The critical opinions had been republished from an article that had appeared in the newspaper the previous day. What made the second article libelous, the court said, was that the reporter "had opportunity to speak with several people" who would have cleared the plaintiff's name before writing the article but had failed to do so. (17)

A 1989 case, Lyons v. R.I. Public Employees Council 94, (18) involved reprints of published articles, one public employees union sued another public employees union contending it was libeled by the distribution of reprints of syndicated newspaper columns during a union election campaign. The plaintiff union claimed that while the information in the original columns was true at the time of publication, by the time the reprints were disseminated, some of the facts no longer were true. (19)

The state Supreme Court, however, ruled that the reprints were accurately dated in type larger than the text and the articles contained historical references indicating that the reprints referred to prior events. (20) In addition, the court said that the reprints were not distributed with actual malice. (21)

Identification

To prove the second element or basic consideration in a defamation case, the plaintiff must show that he or she was actually the person defamed. Thus, the person must be identified. Usually persons who are a part of a large group cannot win a defamation suit because they cannot show they were defamed as individuals.

Most of the time the identification is obvious. However, that was not the situation in three cases heard by courts in Rhode Island.

The Rhode Island Supreme Court dealt with the issue of a plaintiff's responsibility to prove identification in a libel case in 1948 involving a story published in the *Evening Call* in

Woonsocket. The newspaper printed an article based on an anonymous letter it had received from someone claiming to have killed "the wrong man." The right man, the letter said, was "a tall grey haired man who runs a bingo game on Main Street." (22)

Although never named in the article, a man sued the newspaper, saying he had been defamed. The court sent the case back to the lower court because the man had failed to offer proof that he was the man described in the letter even though he was not named. The state Supreme Court said:

> It is too well established to require citation of authority that actionable libel can be constituted by written or printed signs or descriptions provided they are sufficient by themselves to identify the plaintiff as the one concerning whom the defamatory article was published. Where such identification, in the mind of the average reader in the community where the article is circulated, does not appear on the face of the publication, it must be supplied by other proper allegations of fact in an appropriate part of the declaration. (23)

The court referred to that ruling in a 1964 case brought by a letter carrier against a local business. The letter carrier said he was defamed in a letter to the customers of the business which claimed advertisements were not being delivered to some customers due to the fault "of a small number of postal employees." (24) As in the 1948 decision involving the newspaper, the court ruled in the letter carrier case that the plaintiff had provided insufficient facts to prove identification. (25)

In Riverhouse Publishing Company v. Sylvia Porter, the federal court in Rhode Island in 1968 held that a libelous article must refer to "some ascertained or ascertainable person who must be the plaintiff." (26) The court ruled against the plaintiff because Porter in her syndicated column had named neither the publishing company nor the title of a book when she warned readers to beware of a mail solicitation to "leading men all over the U.S. in recent years" to have their names listed in a bio-graphical encyclopedia. (27)

The issue of group libel arose in a case brought by 21 members of a Massachusetts town police department against a Rhode Island newspaper. (28)

A column in the *Woonsocket Call and Evening Reporter* ended with the question: "Is it true that a Bellingham (Massachusetts) cop locked himself and a female companion in the back of a cruiser in a town sandpit and had to radio for help?" The First Circuit Court of Appeals ruled that since the column did not refer to an individual police officer, none of the 21 unnamed officers was libeled. To allow all unnamed members of the group to sue "would chill communication to the marrow," the court said. (29)

Defamatory Communication

The third element a plaintiff in a libel case must prove is that the language is defamatory, either on its face (per se) or by innuendo (per quod).

Rhode Island courts have clearly established that "for a plaintiff to prevail in a libel suit, he/she must prove that the publication was defamatory per se or by reason of its susceptibility of the defamatory meaning attributed to it by way of innuendo. (30) In per se defamation cases, the plaintiff does not have to prove special damages or does not have to show monetary or economic loss. In per quod, the plaintiff, to be successful, must show such a loss occurred.

Words and phrases that most often involved in defamation cases are those stating or suggesting serious moral failings, criminal activities, or incompetence in the plaintiff's professional or business life. Words can be printed or broadcast and can appear in such diverse places as headlines, stories, photo captions, advertisements and memos.

In many states, including Rhode Island, the judge determines whether the words are capable of defamatory meaning,

10

(31) and the jury determines if the person suing was actually defamed. (32)

In 1897, the Rhode Island Supreme Court said that language in a libel case "is not to be forced or tortured...to make it actionable. It is to be taken in its plain and ordinary sense." (33)

Per Se Defamation

One of the earliest libel cases decided by the Rhode Island Supreme Court was in 1897, and it became the basis for decisions in a number of the defamation cases brought before the state courts in the 1970s and 1980s. (34)

In Reid v. Providence Journal Co., the court said:

> Language is not to be forced or tortured in libel cases in order to make it actionable. It is to be taken in its plain and ordinary sense. And, although greater liberality is exercised in the case of words when they are spoken than when they are contained in written or printed articles, yet in both cases the person must be presumed to have used them in their ordinary import in the community in which they are uttered or published.(35)

That definition has prevailed in a number of cases since then. One of the most recent was in 1988 in which the state Supreme Court ruled in favor of the Shell Oil Company.(36) The company was sued by a Rhode Island resident who had received a letter from Shell with the words "Pre cancellation Notice" on the outside of the envelope. The plaintiff claimed the words had libeled him because they announced, at least to his wife and the mailman, that he had failed to pay his credit card bills. (37)

In determining if the statement on the envelope was defamatory, the court cited the Reid definition of language. The court said the envelope did not contain or imply a false statement of fact, because, citing earlier cases, "words alleged to be defamatory must be considered in the context in which they appear." (38)

In two other cases, the state Supreme Court ruled that the language in an alleged defamation was neither per se nor per quod.

The first case was decided by the court in 1970. An obituary notice in a local newspaper that failed to list the wife as a survivor was not libelous per se, and because the plaintiff failed to prove special damages, the court said, the publication could not be considered libel per quod. (39)

The second case, decided in 1985 by the Rhode Island Supreme Court, involved the publication of an annual report of the College of Pharmacy at the University of Rhode Island. The report carried a brief notice that an employee of the college "was terminated...at the end of the academic year." (40) The employee sued the dean of the college for libel.

The state Supreme Court ruled against the employee saying, "In the ordinary sense, an announcement of the termination of an employee, whether printed among other announcements or printed alone, is neither defamatory per se nor defamatory per quod." (41) Again the court applied the definition it set forth in the Reid decision on language "taken in its plain and ordinary sense." (42)

Per Quod Defamation

Per se defamation requires facts, whereas defamation per quod is defamation by innuendo. It needs extrinsic facts. Sometimes, if a plaintiff cannot successfully argue that a communication is defamation per se, he/she may choose to claim it is defamation per quod.

Most of the court's recent rulings on innuendo have stemmed from a 1931 case, Ross v. Providence Journal Company. (43) Ross sued the newspaper for defamation over an article and its headline, which read "Police Inspectors Seeking Max Ross." The story explained that Ross' car had been stolen the previous night and later was found burned. (44)

In his defamation suit, Ross claimed that a reader could infer from the headline and the story that he was being sought by the police for stealing and destroying his car. (45) The court considered the headline and the article as a whole and ruled for the newspaper, saying that Ross, the plaintiff, "had improperly enlarged the natural meaning of the words of the article by the introduction of new matter in the innuendos." (46)

In Bray v. Providence Journal Company, the court, in 1966, referred to several earlier rulings (47) when it said that the purpose of an innuendo is to define the defamatory meaning of words which may be equivocal, but "it cannot be used to intro-duce new matter or to enlarge the meaning of the words to give language a construction it will not bear." (48)

Bray was a school teacher and president elect of the Pawtucket Teachers' Alliance who sued the *Providence Jour-nal* for alleged libel in the headline, "Testimony Challenged Al-liance Head `Lied,' Dr. Savoie Declares." The court said that the headline "was not in its entirety reasonably capable of con-veying to the ordinary mind the defamatory meaning alleged in the innuendo" of the headline. (49)

In a 1975 decision by the U.S. Court of Appeals, First Circuit, affirming a decision by the federal district court in Provi-dence, the appeals court said it was reluctant to entertain libel suits dependent upon a precise construction of a newspaper's technical, legal terminology. (50)

In Lambert v. Providence Journal Company, Lambert was the owner of a cafe in Fall River, Massachusetts, who was charged with shooting and killing a patron. Several stories were published in *The Providence Journal* concerning the shoot-ing. Lambert sued the newspaper for libel, claiming the use of language in the stories libeled him by innuendo. (He later was acquitted of the charge.) (51)

Lambert said the newspaper's characterization of the man killed as "the murder victim" and the incident itself as "a murder" constituted editorial comment and imputed his guilt. Such neutral words as "shooting death," "homicide" or "killing" should have been used in the articles, he said. To support his construction, he submitted depositions of three community residents who testified that such had been their "fair," "plain" and "ordinary" understanding of the articles in question. (52)

The Rhode Island Supreme Court ruled that the language used in the articles was "not reasonably conveying the defamatory meaning the plaintiff alleged." (53) The word "murder" was used interchangeably throughout the articles with the terms "fatal shooting," "shooting death" and "homicide" often in the same sentences, the court noted. (54) In explaining its ruling, the court said:

> In this context, the term clearly is chosen solely for variety's sake and merely echoes the report of the charges levelled against Lambert without implying their truthfulness....The innuendo cannot be used to enlarge the natural meaning of the words actually used... None of the articles could be construed to impute guilt without such enlargement. (55)

The court concluded that despite the *Journal's* "loose use of the word 'murder', we think only 'supersensitive persons, with morbid imaginations' could discover in any of these articles the assertion that Lambert was guilty of murder." (56)

Fault: Defining the Alleged Defamed Person

It is important in a defamation case for the court to determine whether the person alleging defamation is a public official, a public figure or a private person. In Rhode Island a public official or a public figure must show that the communicator (the defendant) acted with "actual malice." (57)

In contrast, Rhode Island courts have said that a private individual suing for defamation is held only to ordinary standards of negligence. (58)

It is generally less difficult for a plaintiff to prove communicator negligence than to prove "actual malice." Therefore, it is in the best interests of the alleged defamed person to be considered a private person. It is in the communicator's best interest for the alleged defamed person to be considered a public figure or official.

It should be noted that before 1964, an alleged defamed person, regardless of whether he or she was a public or a private person, had only to prove negligence. However, that year the United States Supreme Court made it much more difficult for public officials to prove defamation. In what the court called an effort "to protect uninhibited, robust, and wide open" (59) debate, it ruled in New York Times v. Sullivan that public officials suing the media for statements about their official conduct had to prove that the defamation was published with knowing falsehood or reckless disregard for the truth. This became known as "New York Times actual malice."

In 1967 the Supreme Court said that public figures as well as public officials must prove "actual malice" in a libel suit (60). Seven years later the high court defined a public figure as either a person of widespread fame or notoriety or a person who has injected himself or herself into a debate about a controversial public issue for a purpose of affecting the outcome. (61)

Public Officials

Since 1964, the Rhode Island Supreme Court has ruled on two cases both in the 1980s in which the alleged defamed persons were public officials. One was a broadcast defamation case, the other involved a newspaper. In neither case did the alleged defamed person prevail.

In Hawkins v. Oden, a member of the state Senate brought defamation action against the host of a radio talk show and the show's producer. Citing New York Times v. Sullivan and Gertz v. Welch, the court upheld a lower court's ruling that the senator was a public official "for the purpose of the *New York Times* defamation test." (62) The senator sued because of statements made by the talk show host during a call in program concerning the state's lease of a building in which the senator had a financial interest.

The talk show host characterized the senator's conduct in the affair "as reaching into the public till with both hands" and "stealing public money." The court said that was because the lease transaction and the senator's part in it were "extensively detailed by newspaper and radio stories," (63), and because the person alleging defamation was a state senator and majority leader of that body, his claim of libel was not actionable under the *New York Times* standard. (64)

In Hall v. Rogers, the state's high court ruled that two police officers a father and son were public officials. (65) The two men brought a defamation suit against *The Providence Journal* and one of its reporters for alleged defamatory statements in an article published in the newspaper concerning "irregularities" in the way the two men performed their jobs. (66) In applying the Times v. Sullivan ruling, the Rhode Island high court said:

> ... the plaintiffs contention that Hall Sr.'s status as a sergeant and Hall Jr.'s status as a special police officer do not render them qualified candidates for 'public official' status are respectfully without merit. (67)

Public Figures

In 1980, the Rhode Island Supreme Court set forth the guidelines based on the *New York Times* and Gertz decisions in DeCarvalho v. daSilva. (68) These guidelines continue to be used by the state courts for defining a public figure.

DeCarvalho, the plaintiff, was an attorney and honorary Portuguese Consul General for Rhode Island. In this capacity he annually signed visas for 300 400 Portuguese nationals living in Rhode Island who were travelling to the Azores and participated in activities of interest to the local Portuguese community, between 70,000 and 100,000 people. During this time he and two associates helped to obtain for a fee immigration documents for residents of the Azores to work in the United States. Such assistance was a violation of a Portuguese statute. A Portuguese trial court in the Azores found the three men guilty of violating the statute and imposed a fine. DeCarvalho, because of his presumed knowledge of Portuguese law, was the only one required to pay a fine. He appealed to the Supreme Court of Portugal which upheld the lower court's decision. (69)

DaSilva, a physician who had been active for many years in local Portuguese affairs, became aware of DeCarvalho's actions and subsequent fine. DaSilva then published articles critical of DeCarvalho in a Portuguese language publication which DeCarvalho said defamed him. DaSilva also broadcast statements which DeCarvalho said defamed him over a Newport, R.I. radio station. The articles and broadcasts "exaggerated the incident all out of proportion...and were...coupled with inaccuracies and certain statements of fact which were wrong," the plaintiff claimed. (70)

The Rhode Isand Supreme Court dealt with two important issues raised in the case. One concerned the plaintiff DeCarvalho's claim that daSilva was not "a professional member of the news media" and did not deserve protection under the New York Times standard. (71) To this, the court said:

> This contention raises many types of equal protection problems. Defining professional members of the media would be a difficult task indeed. This would require drawing distinctions between free lance writers and the occasional author of a book, article, or pamphlet on the one hand and regularly employed agents of a great metropolitan daily newspaper or broadcasting syndicate on the other. As far as we are aware, the freedom of the press enshrined in the First Amendment

was designed to apply to the lonely pamphleteer as well as
to the (then unknown) syndicated columnist. (72)

The court then looked at the status of the plaintiff
DeCarvalho. The judge in the lower court ruled him a public
figure. (73) The high court confirmed this, noting that
DeCarvalho was "a pervasive public figure" in the Portuguese
community and "therefore had the burden to prove that the
allegedly defamatory material was published by the defendant
doctor with knowledge that the defamatory statement was false
or with reckless disregard..." (74)

More recently, the Rhode Island Supreme Court has ruled
in three cases which also focused on the public figure status of
the plaintiff in a defamatory action.

Citing the decision in DeCarvalho v. daSilva, the state
Supreme Court in 1985 said that the lower court had been correct in ruling that a real estate developer, the plaintiff in Martin
v. Wilson, had attained "public figure" status in the village where
the allegedly libelous newspaper article was circulated. The
court said that he had acquired many properties in the center of
the village, and he had appeared numerous times before local
regulatory agencies to secure appropriate permits to proceed
with various plans. (75)

The plaintiff challenged his designation as a public figure
on the grounds that the newspaper also circulated widely outside the village and that his "mere ownership of property" in
the village and the village residents' knowledge of him "did not
justify the trial justice's conclusion that (he) in the circumstances
of this case, was a public figure." The court disagreed with
both contentions. (76)

A year later, in Major v. Drapeau, the court said that the
director of a state funded drug rehabilitation program made
himself a public figure by actively seeking publicity by issuing
statements to the press. He also requested a newspaper reporter be present when the director examined the records of a

18

private agency under contract to the state. (77) He was unable to prove that published statements by the defendants, members of the state legislature, were made with "actual malice." (78)

In Capuano v. Outlet Co., the Rhode Island Supreme Court upheld the lower court's ruling that the owners of a trash hauling company were "limited public figures." The court based its 1990 decision on the fact that the men had been the subject of numerous newspaper stories and had, from time to time, granted interviews to the local media in connection with controversies surrounding their business. (79)

The First Circuit U.S. Court of Appeals ruled in 1987 that the owner of a time share resort on Block Island, off the southern shore of the state, was a public figure for at least the limited purpose of a controversy surrounding the resort which had been the subject of an article in the island's weekly newspaper. (80)

In a 1995 case involving a local manufacturer who sued the magazine *Consumer Reports*, (81) the U.S. District Court in Rhode Island ruled the manufacturer a "limited purpose public figure" because the company actively solicited independent product testing and reviews and used the reviews in its marketing. (82)

Private Persons

The state's high court had little problem in ruling that the physician in Healey v. New England Newspapers, Inc. was a private figure. (82) The court said the controversy that resulted in the defamation did not involve the physician's role as the president of the board of directors of the local YMCA or the public controversy in which the board was involved at the time. Rather, the statements that appeared in the newspaper related to his role as a physician, "a reference to his private life, not his public life." (83)

Levels of Proof Needed for Damages

Actual Malice Test

Public officials and public figures cannot recover actual or compensatory damages for defamatory falsehoods unless they can prove the statement was published with "actual malice"—knowledge on the part of the communicator (defendant) that the statement was false—or published with reckless disregard of whether it was true or false. Actual malice must be proved by clear and convincing evidence. (84)

The state courts have held that compensatory damages may be awarded based upon the mental anguish and humiliation experienced as a result of a defamatory statement. (85)

In cases where the plaintiff has been determined to be a public official or a public figure, Rhode Island courts have followed closely the rulings in New York Times v. Sullivan and Gertz v. Welch. (86) The federal court in Rhode Island has continued to look to Gertz v. Welch as was shown in the Quantum Electronics v. Consumers Union case (87) when it said the plaintiff, a limited purpose public figure, must prove with "clear and convincing evidence" that the defamatory falsehood was made with "knowledge of its falsity or with a reckless disregard for the truth." (88)

Actual malice, however, is not synonymous with common law spite or ill will, and, in general, proof of a corrupt motive, spite, ill will or general hostility will not satisfy the *New York Times* standard. (89) The test for "actual malice" is a subjective one which requires the jury to determine the state of mind of the defendant (communicator) at the time he or she published the articles or made the broadcast in question. (90)

In addition, there must be sufficient evidence to permit the jury to conclude that the defendant in fact entertained serious doubts as to the truth of his or her publication. Publishing with such doubts, the Rhode Island courts have said, shows reckless disregard for the truth or falsity and demonstrates to the court that the article was published or broadcast with "actual malice." (91)

Failure to verify information standing alone does not constitute recklessness. As long as the sources of the alleged libelous material appeared reliable, and the defendant had no doubts about its accuracy, even if a more thorough investigation might have uncovered the error, the courts have found insufficient evidence of malice. (92)

In Hall v. Rogers, the court said that the source of the alleged libelous material was the assistant mayor of East Providence and a member of the city council, who had been used as a reliable source in published articles in the past. Thus, the court said, the reporter had no reason to doubt the truth of the official's statements. Since he was considered a reliable source, the reporter "had conducted herself properly by relying on the information conveyed to her and the trial justice was correct in his determination that there was no factual dispute in regard to actual malice as defined in New York Times Co." The plaintiff's appeal was denied. (93)

But publication of false or baseless rumors makes the publisher responsible under the "actual malice" test. (94)

In Martin v. Wilson, the state Supreme Court overturned a ruling by the Superior Court. In the lower court, the judge had told the jury that as a matter of law if rumors, such as those in the case at bar (ie. that the plaintiff, a developer, had been guilty of arson) were current at or before the time of publication, the newspaper could publish them with impunity. For the plaintiff to prevail, he would have to prove there were no such rumors. (95) The Supreme Court disagreed, saying that was "not an appropriate application of the New York Times 'actual malice' test." (96)

The court noted that even if the reporter or publisher might not have had actual knowledge of the falsity of the rumors, either one of them "certainly had sufficient doubts about their truth to make it a question of fact about whether the statements had been published with reckless disregard of whether they were false or not." (97)

Negligence Test

In Rhode Island a private individual suing for defamation is held only to the ordinary standard of negligence under both federal and state law. (98)

In DeCarvalho v. daSilva the court interpreted the U.S. Supreme Court's restrictions in respect to allowing private figures to recover damages for defamatory publications:

> ...states may apply their own laws in respect to the publishing of defamatory materials, except that liability may not be established without fault (a concept that indicates that at least ordinary negligence be shown.) (99)

Recovery of damages by private persons must be limited on the ordinary negligence standard to actual damages incurred. The state Supreme Court has said that if punitive damages (those which punish a publication rather than compensate the plaintiff) are to be awarded, then the "actual malice" element must be shown by "clear and convincing evidence." (100)

Additional Constraints for the Alleged Defamed Person
Common Law and Other Defenses

Truth

Truth as a defense in a libel case appears in the state Constitution: "... in all trials for libel, both civil and criminal, the truth, unless published from malicious motives, shall be sufficient defense to the person charged." (101)

The defense also is guaranteed by state statute. (102)

In 1989, the state Supreme Court said that truth is a complete defense in an action for libel "no matter how much harm is done by the statements," and emphasized that the plaintiff has the burden of establishing that the publication is false. (103) The court added that "so long as the gist or the sting of the publication is true, the publication is not false." (104)

Privileges

Absolute Privilege: Absolute privilege allows government officials, communicating in their professional capacity, to speak out without fear of being sued for defamation. Discussions between employer and employee also are privileged as are personnel recommendations by an employer about an employee.

The Rhode Island Constitution specifically protects the speech of legislators: "For any speech in debate in either house, no member shall be questioned in any other place." (105)

In addition the federal court in Rhode Island has said that libelous matters filed in judicial proceedings where statements are material to the case fall under absolute privilege. (106)

Qualified Privilege: In Martin v. Wilson, the state Supreme Court said that the common law privilege of fair report allows journalists to report on meetings of publicly elected or appointed bodies so long as the published material portrays fair and accurate accounts of public meetings and judicial proceedings even when an individual is defamed during the proceeding or action. (107)

However, the court noted, this privilege does not abrogate the policy of protecting a person's reputation. Rather it subordinates it to the public's interest in the information about official proceedings and public meetings. (108)

Publishing rumors, however, is not privileged. In Martin v. Wilson, the court pointed out that with public meetings a person against whom defamatory statements are aimed "may attend such gatherings and defend against such attacks." The same is true in a judicial proceeding if a person is defamed through cross examination. "The opportunity exists for the one defamed to respond to rebut the defamation." But the court found no similar policy to protect the repetition of rumors. (109)

> The spreading of rumors does not give the person defamed by them the opportunity to rebut the underlying allegations of the rumor. To attempt to defend against a rumor is not unlike attempting to joust with a cloud. (110)

Employer employee privilege was examined in a recent case in Rhode Island. In 1987, the state Supreme Court said that communication between a personnel administrator and an employee's immediate supervisor about the reasons for the employee's termination fell under the scope of qualified privilege for defamation action. (111)

Broadcast Privilege: While broadcast owners and employees can be held accountable for defamatory statements they make over the air (112), the stations have an absolute privilege for defamatory remarks made by political candidates during time provided under the equal opportunities provision of the Federal Communication Act. (113)

Neutral Reportage: A doctrine called neutral reportage allows journalists to report newsworthy statements made by reliable sources even if the reporter doubts the accuracy of the information. (114) Only a few courts have adopted the doctrine. In a footnote to the Martin v. Wilson decision, the Rhode Island Supreme Court said it was "not entirely convinced of the soundness" of the doctrine. (115)

> The question of whether material is published with knowledge of falsity or reckless disregard of whether it is true or false in substance would require the trier of fact to consider the credibility or responsibility of the source upon which the publication is based. Therefore, it is questionable whether an additional layer of privilege is required. (116)

Instead, the court said, it would await a case which carefully presented that question of added privilege before deciding whether to accept or reject the doctrine of neutral reportage. (117)

Opinion

Constitutionally protected opinion was a successful defense in two recent cases heard by the federal court, McCabe v. Rattiner (118) and Fudge v. Penthouse. (119) Rattiner, the publisher of a weekly newspaper circulated on Block Island, wrote an article about a real estate time sharing business on the island which began on page one of the newspaper. The word "scam" appeared as the jump line (the inside page headline) over the article which was written in a first person, narrative style. (120) The First Circuit U.S. Court of Appeals looked at the article as a whole and the context in which the "scam" was used and ruled that it was a protected statement of opinion under the U.S. Constitution. (121)

In Fudge v. Penthouse the appeals court said that the men's magazine's use of the word "amazon" to describe some schoolgirls was not an assertion of fact but "instead a statement of constitutionally protected opinion." (122)

The federal court in Rhode Island ruled in 1995 that a statement in the form of opinion may be defamatory and therefore actionalbe "if an donly if it implies the allegation of undisclosed defamatory facts as the basis for the opinion." (123)

Consent

Rhode Island courts have allowed the defense of consent. In Capuano v. The Outlet Company, the Supreme Court determined that the owners of waste collection and disposal companies were "public figures" in part because they had consented to be interviewed by the media or made statements to members of the media about their businesses as they related to a controversy about the businesses and their alleged relationship to organized crime. (124)

Death and Defamation

In 1974 the state legislature enacted a that would allow the family or the estate of a person allegedly defamed in his or her obituary or in similar accounts published within three months of the person's death to sue the newspaper or broadcast station carrying the article. The law states that such legal action must begin within one year after the death of the person. If the suit is successful, any damages retrieved would be awarded to the beneficiaries. (120)

Time Limitation

Under Rhode Island law, a person who believes he or she has been slandered must initiate legal action within one year after the words were spoken. (121) The time limitation for bringing a libel action is three years. In Mikaelian v. Drug Abuse Unit, the state Supreme Court ruled that the three year limitation period begins when the alleged materials were originally written and published. This case involved a memorandum and a letter. (122)

Criminal Indictment for Libel

Rhode Island has a criminal indictment for libel, although it has not been used in recent times. Just as a person can be indicted for larceny, forgery or manslaughter or any other crime, so a person or publication can be indicted by a grand jury for criminal libel. The indictment form, however, specifies that the published libel must be in the form of "a letter, book, picture, or as the case may be the particulars should specify the pages and lines constituting the libel, when necessary, as where it is contained in book or pamphlet." (123)

Endnotes

1. Dexter v. Spear, Fed. Cas. No. 3,867, 4 Mason, 115 (Fed. Cir.Ct. App., RI 1825).

2. Reid et al. v. Providence Journal Co., 37 A. 637 (RI 1897).

3. Elias v. Youngken, 493 A. 2d 158 (RI 1985).

4. Hawkins v. Oden, 459 A. 2d 485 (RI 1983).

5. The Restatement (Second) Torts 568A (1977).

6. RI Gen. Laws, 9 6 9.

7. RI Gen. Laws, 10 7 1 5.

8. Healey v. New England Newspapers, 555 A. 2d 321 (RI 1989).

9. Gaudette v. Carter, 214 A. 2d 197 (RI 1965). There have been numerous cases in Rhode Island involving free speech. Socha v. National Association of Letter Carriers, 883 F. Supp.. 790 (DRI 1995) for instance, reaffirmed Gaudette that publication requires that the defamatory words be communicated to a third person and understood by him or her. Because this is a book aimed at media professionals, those cases are not included. In addition to free speech protection in the state constitution, Rhode Island has a "hateful speech" law (R.I. Gen. Law 11 53 1,2,3) which says that anyone found guilty of terrorizing or intimidating another person through speech or physical acts can be fined or imprisoned.

10. Lonardo v. Quaranta, 205 A. 2d 838 (RI 1964).

11. 459 A. 2d 485.

12. Martin v. Wilson, 497 A. 2d 322 (RI 1985).

13. Cianci v. New Times Publishing Co., 639 F. 2d 54, 60 61 (2d Cir. 1980); Metcalf v. The Times Publishing Co., 40 A. 864 (RI 1898).

14. 497 A. 2d 327.

15. Id. at 323.

16. 555 A. 2d 328.

17. Id. at 328.

18. Lyons v. R.I. Public Employees Council 94, 559 A. 2d 130 (RI 1989).

19. Id.

20. Id. at 131.

21. Id.

22. Carey v. Evening Call Pub. Co., 62 A. 2d, 327 (RI 1948).

23. Id. at 330.

24. Connery v. Kalian, 205 A. 2d 587 (RI 1964).

25. Id.

26. 287 F. Supp. 1.

27. Id. at 3.

28. Arcand et al., v. The Evening Call Publishing Company, 567 F. 2d 1163 (1st Cir. 1977) .

29. Id. at 1165.

30. Andoscia v. Coady, 310 A. 2d 481 (RI 1965).

31. Id.

32. Ross v. Providence Journal Co., 154 A. 563 (RI 1931).

33. Reid v. Providence Journal Co., 37 A. 637, 638 (RI 1897).

34. Id at 637.

35. Id.

36. McCann v. Shell Oil Co., 551 A. 2d 696 (RI 1988).

37. Id at 698.

38. Id.

39. Barrett v. Barrett, 271 A. 2d 825 (RI 1970).

40. Elias v. Youngken, 493 A. 2d 160.

41. Id at 161.

42. Id.

43. Ross v. Providence Journal Co., 154 A., 562 (RI 1931).

44. Id at 562, 563.

45. Id at 562.

46. Id at 563.

47. Bray v. Providence Journal Co., 220 A. 2d 531 (RI 1966).

48. Id. at 534.

49. Id at 531.

50. Lambert v. Providence Journal Co., 508 F. 2d 659 (First Cir., 1975).

51. Id at 658.

52. Id.

53. Id.

54. Id.

55. Id at 659.

56. Id.

57. DeCarvalho v. daSilva, 414 A.2d 807, 814 (RI 1980).

58. Capuano v. The Outlet Company, 579 A.2d 469 (RI 1990).

59. New York Times Co. v. Sullivan, 376 US 270 (US Sup. Ct. 1964). The U.S. District Court in Rhode Island cited the "robust debate" statement in the Times v. Sullivan decision in 1989 when it ruled in Providence Journal Company v. Newton and Kass v. Newton (723 F. Supp. 846). The District Court said that confidentiality requirement of the state's government ethics law (R.I. Gen. Law 36 14 5), which prohibited all public discussion of the existence or content of an ethics complaint against a public official, was a "content based" restriction on "political speech" protected by the First Amendment.

60. Curtis Pub. Co. v. Butts, 388 US 130 (US Sup. Ct. 1967).

61. Gertz v. Robert Welch, Inc., 418 US 325 (US Sup. Ct. 1974). (In this landmark case, the U.S. Supreme Court divided public figures into two categories: persons of widespread fame or notoriety, and persons who have injected themselves into a debate about a controversial public issue for the purpose of affecting the outcome.)

62. 459 A. 2d 482.

63. Id at 483.

64. Id at 482.

65. Hall v. Rogers, 490 A.2d 502 (RI 1985).

66. Id at 503.

67. Id at 506.

68. 414 A. 2d 806.

69. Id at 808.

70. Id at 809.

71. Id at 813.

72. DeCarvalho v. daSilva, 414 A.2d 813 (RI 1980).

73. Id.

74. Id at 807.

75. 497 A.2d 322, 323.

76. Id at 325,326.

77. Major v. Drapeau, 507 A.2d 941 (RI 1986).

78. Id at 942.

79. Capuano et al. v. The Outlet Company, 579 A.2d 471 (RI 1990).

80. McCabe et al. v. Rattiner et al., 814 F. 2d 839 (First Cir., 1987).

81. Quantum Electronics Corps. v. Consumers Union, 881 F. Supp. 753 (DRI 1995).

82. Id. at 765, citing 418 US 345 (U.S. Sup. Ct. 1974).

83. 555 A.2d 321.

84. Id at 325.

85. 507 A.2d 938.

86. 555 A.2d 327.

87. 881 F. Supp. 753 (DRI 1995). Also refer. to 414 A.2d 806; 490 A.2d 502; 507 A.2d 938; 579 A.2d 469.

88. 881 F. Supp. 763.

89. 507 A.2d 941.

90. 414 A.2d 814. In Capuano v. Outlet, (579 A.2d 469, 470) the state Supreme Court said that defamation plaintiffs need not engage in futile preliminary investigations and depositions before being permitted to ask questions directly of those whose "knowledge and state of mind are critical to the determination of the issue of 'actual' malice.

91. Id at 812.

92. 490 A.2d 505.

93. Id at 506.

94. 497 A.2d 327.

95. Id.

96. Id at 328.

97. Id.

98. 579 A.2d 469.

99. 414 A.2d 812.

100. Id at 813.

101. RI Constitution, Art. I, Sec. 20.

102. R.I. Gen. Laws, 9 6 9.

103. 555 A.2d 325.

104. Id.

105. R.I. Constitution, Art. VI, Sec. 5. (R.I. Gen. Law 8 16 11 makes any papers filed with or testimony given before the Commission on Judicial Tenure and Discipline privileged in any action for defamation.

106. Kissell v. Dunn, 793 F. Supp. 389 (DRI 1992).

107. 497 A.2d 328.

108. Id.

109. Id at 329.

110. Id.

111. DiBiasio v. Brown and Sharpe, 525 A.2d 489.

112. 459 A.2d 485.

113. Fed. Comm. Act, Sec. 315 (a).

114. Edwards v. National Audubon Society, Inc., 556 F. 2d

115. 497 A.2d 330.

116. Id.

117. Id.

118. 814 F.2d 839.

119. Fudge v. Penthouse International, Ltd. 840 F.2d 1012 (First Cir. 1988).

120. 814 F.2d 843.

121. Id. at 442, 443.

122. 840 F.2d 1012.

123. 863 F. Supp. 806.

124. 579 A.2d 469.

125. R.I. Gen. Laws, 10 7.1 1,2, 1974.

126. R.I. Gen. Laws. 9 1 14 (a).

127. Mikaelian v. Drug Abuse Unit, 501 A.2d 721 (RI 1985).

128. Form 16, Superior Court Rules of Criminal Procedure.

Invasion of Privacy in Rhode Island

Unlike defamation, which has long been defined in law, the right of privacy is a relatively new area of media law in the United States.

Invasion of the right to privacy as a tort can be traced to an article in the Harvard Law Review in 1890, by two Boston lawyers, Samuel Warren and Louis Brandeis, who later became a justice of the United States Supreme Court. (1) In the article, the two men concluded that a common law right to privacy, essentially a right "to be let alone," was entitled to explicit recognition because the substance of the right already was protected under the law of property, defamation and contracts. (2)

Since that article appeared, the courts have gradually developed a common law right to privacy. In 1977 the American Law Institute attempted to present an orderly statement of the four categories of the common law of privacy in the *Restatement of the Law of Torts*. (3) Three years later, the Rhode Island General Assembly (the legislature) adopted a Privacy Law (4) which closely parallels the law outlined in the *Restatement.*

The Rhode Island law recognizes all four categories of invasion of privacy. They are:

(a) Unreasonable intrusion upon one's physical solitude or seclusion.

(b) Appropriation of one's name or likeness.

(c) Unreasonable publicity to one's private life.

(d) Publicity that places one in a false light before the public. (5)

Although the state legislature did not pass a comprehensive privacy law until 1980, the first privacy case heard in the state was in 1909 when the Rhode Island Supreme Court ruled that a constitutional "right to be let alone" in fact referred to the right to be free from bodily injury or from a reasonable fear of such injury but not a right to be free from "public comment." (6) Henry v. Cherry & Webb involved the publication of the plaintiff's photograph in a newspaper advertisement without his consent. He claimed that as a result, he had been held up to public ridicule and had suffered mental distress. (7) The court said there was no common law right of privacy entitling a person to recover damages for mental suffering caused by the publication. (8)

In 1972, the federal district court in Rhode Island chastised the state for its lack of a privacy law. (9) "Rhode Island last rejected the right of privacy in the Henry case in 1909. Since then Rhode Island case law has been entirely silent on the subject, and the state legislature has likewise failed to enact a statute regarding the right of privacy." (10) Three months later, the state's General Assembly enacted a law that allowed a plaintiff injunctive relief and damages when his or her name, portrait or photograph were used for advertising or trade purposes without the person's written consent. (11)

The next privacy related case came before the courts in Rhode Island in the late 1970s, when the owner of several multi family dwellings sought an injunction and damages for alleged invasion of privacy and the infliction of emotional distress because a local community action group was picketing his place of worship and at his fraternal association to bring pressure on him to improve the properties. (12) The landlord said the picketing and the distribution of leaflets accusing him of "slumlandlordism" had placed him in a false light. (13)

Although the state Supreme Court ruled that the landlord had no cause of action, (14) it did take the opportunity to urge the General Assembly to enact a privacy law. (15) In 1980, the legislature did so.

Intrusion

Intrusion is the right to be secure from unreasonable intrusion upon one's physical solitude or seclusion. (16)

In the common law of privacy, intrusion is a highly physical, electronic or mechanical invasion of another's solitude or seclusion. (17)

Under Rhode Island law, for a plaintiff to recover damages for violation of this right, he or she must prove:

(a) It was an invasion of something that is entitled to be private or would be expected to be private. (18)

(b) Such an invasion was or is offensive or objectionable to a reasonable person. (19)

However, the person who discloses the information need not benefit from such disclosure. (20)

Kinds of Intrusion

Intrusion into Public and Quasi Public Places

Under common law, a person can expect little privacy in a public place, such as on the sidewalk or the street. No intrusion exists in photographing a person on a public thoroughfare or in a public park. (21)

However, a photographer could invade a person's privacy in a public place if he or she captured the person in an embarrassing situation. The *Restatement's* classic example is the woman who visits the fun house at an amusement park and a jet of compressed air blows her skirt over her head and reveals her underwear. If she were photographed in that position, the photographer would have invaded her privacy. (22) The courts are divided on whether or not photographers and interviewers have a right to intrude on diners in a restaurant. (23)

Intrusion into Private Places and Concerns

In Russell v. Salve Regina College, the First Circuit Court of Appeals upheld a decision of the federal district court that under Rhode Island's privacy law the college had not invaded the privacy of Sharon Russell, a nursing student, by continually inquiring into her weight loss progress. The student had been deemed overweight by the college's nursing program. In its decision, the Appeals Court noted that the state statute covers only "physical solitude or seclusion," and that the only area "invaded" was Russell's psyche.(24)

According to the *Restatement,* peeping into windows with binoculars or tapping a person's telephone, which is considered third party monitoring, is an intrusion (25), as is examining a person's private concerns by opening a wallet or his or her personal mail, or examining a person's bank account. (26)

There is no invasion in examining public records or documents, including those that the plaintiff is required to keep available for inspection. (27) The Rhode Island Supreme Court said that a record of recently divorced persons available from the Family Court was public and open for inspection. (28)

Invasion may be by physical intrusion into a place in which the plaintiff has secluded himself or herself, such as a defendant forcing his or her way into the plaintiff's hotel room or entering the plaintiff's house over his or her objections. (29)

In 1996 the Rhode Island Supreme Court said that a local family that sued a television station for invasion of privacy (30) after a reporter from the station telephoned the husband who was preparing to commit suicide and interviewed him did not invade the privacy of the husband who killed himself a short time later because the right to privacy dies with the person. (31) The court also said the television station did not invade the privacy of the family because "one telephone call by a reporter did not invade any area of the family's seclusion that could reasonably have been expected to remain private." (32)

Highly Offensive Issue

Under the Rhode Island privacy law, if a person believes his or her physical solitude or seclusion has been invaded, that person must be able to prove that the invasion was so great that it would be considered offensive or objectionable to a reasonable person. (33)

According to the *Restatement,* intrusion does not exist if a reporter knocks on someone's door for an interview or someone calls a person on the telephone several times to collect payment for a debt. (34) However, a person's privacy is invaded when the knocking on the door or the telephone calls "are repeated with such persistence and frequency as to amount to hounding." (35)

Appropriation

The law of appropriation is the oldest in the four areas of privacy invasion, dating to 1903 when New York enacted the country's first privacy law, covering only appropriation. (36)

Under Rhode Island's privacy law, an individual has a right to be secure from the appropriation of his or her name or likeness. To recover, the person must establish that the appropriation was done without his or her permission and that someone else benefited from the act. (37) The federal district court in Rhode Island has ruled that the appropriation must be for noncommercial purposes to be legal. (38)

A separate law (39), enacted in 1972, eight years before the General Assembly approved the privacy law, has been interpreted by the federal court to cover appropriation of a person's likeness or name for commercial purposes. (40) Under this law, if a person's name, portrait or picture is used within the state for advertising purposes or for purposes of trade without the person's written consent, he or she may request injunctive relief from the state's Superior Court and may collect damages for any injuries sustained through the unauthorized use. (41)

Protected under the law is a photographer who exhibits photos at his or her studio unless the person in the photographs gives written notice objecting to the use of his or her likeness. (42) Not protected are those persons who sell their names, portraits or pictures for use in advertisements of a product, or an author, composer or artist who allows his or her name or likeness to be used in connection with his or her work. (43)

In 1988, in Mendonsa v. Time, Inc., (44) the U.S. District Court in Rhode Island attempted to interpret both state statutes relating to appropriation. A photograph taken by Alfred Eisenstadt on V J Day, August 14, 1945, was published the following week in *Life* magazine. The photograph shows a sailor bent over, a portion of his face visible, kissing a nurse in New York City. Mendonsa claimed he was the sailor. The photograph was reprinted several times over the years in *Life* and other publications. In 1980, Life asked individuals claiming to be the sailor to contact the magazine. Mendonsa said he did so, but *Life* made no formal attempt to identify the sailor. In 1987, the magazine ran an advertisement offering to sell copies of the photo to its readers for $1,600. Soon after that, Mendonsa sued the magazine's parent company, Time, Inc. (45)

In deciding the case, the federal court said it had to interpret the two appropriation laws in Rhode Island in such a way that their purposes did not overlap. (46) It ruled that Mendonsa had prevailed in his claim for the misappropriation of his likeness for commercial purposes under the 1972 statute but had failed to state a cause of action under the noncommercial appropriation section of the state's privacy law. (47)

Newsworthiness

The court explained that the first publication, and even subsequent publications, of the photo were protected because they could be deemed newsworthy. But when Time offered the photo for sale, it clearly became "for purposes of trade." (48)

In deciding Mendonsa, the federal court noted that New York courts had consistently emphasized that activities involving the dissemination of news or information concerning matters of public interest are privileged and do not fall within "the purposes of trade." This would apply, for instance, to the use of a name or a picture in a newspaper, magazine, or newsreel, in connection with an item of news of a person who is newsworthy. (49)

The scope of the subject matter which may be considered of "public interest" and "newsworthy" has been defined in liberal and far reaching terms, the Mendonsa court said. (50) (There are limitations.) This privilege, however, does not extend to the commercialization of a personality through a form of treatment distinct from the dissemination of news or information. (51)

For example, a movie company filmed a picture entitled "Sightseeing in New York with Nick and Tony" which it distributed to various movie theaters. Six seconds of the film consisted of closeup, full sized views of a street vendor selling bread and rolls. A New York court held that the vendor's picture had been used for "trade purposes." (52)

Damages

The 1972 Rhode Island statute (misappropriation for commercial purposes) allows successful plaintiffs to recover damages for any injuries sustained by the unauthorized use of their likeness. And if the defendant knowingly misappropriates the person's name, portrait or picture, the court may award the plaintiff treble the amount of damages sustained. (53)

Under the appropriation section of the privacy law, the court may award "reasonable attorney's fees and court costs" to the prevailing party in the suit. (54)

Private Facts

According to the Rhode Island law, a person has a right to be secure from unreasonable publicity given to his or her private life. (55) There must be some publication of a private fact. (56) And the fact must be one which would be offensive or objectionable to a reasonable person of ordinary sensibilities. (57) The discloser of the fact need not benefit in any way for the publication of the fact to be an unreasonable invasion. (58)

Publicity Requirement

Publicity means the matter must be made public by being communicated to the public at large or to so many persons that the matter must be regarded as substantially certain to become one of public knowledge. It can be written or oral. (59) Unlike defamation, where the alleged defamatory information need be communicated only to a third party to make it actionable, "it is not an invasion of privacy to communicate a fact concerning a person's private life to a single person or even to a small group of people." (60)

But publishing a private fact in a newspaper or magazine, even of small circulation, is sufficient to be considered publicity. (61)

Private Matters

It is not an invasion of privacy to give publicity to information about a person that already is public knowledge. This includes matters of public record, such as date of birth, the fact of marriage, a military record, or that a person was admitted to the practice of medicine or failed in a lawsuit. (62)

The Rhode Island privacy law specifically exempts any public records that are open by statute. (63) In 1991, the state Supreme Court ruled that Rhode Island's Privacy Act does not apply to the records of the Family Court concerning divorce.

(64) The court said, "The statutory right to privacy does not extend to those records deemed public, and (the) records in question were public." (65)

There is no invasion for giving further publicity to "what a person normally leaves open to the public eye." *The Restatement* uses as an example a person walking down the street who should expect that if his or her photograph is taken, it could be published or broadcast. (66)

A photograph taken in a private place and made public without the person's consent is an invasion of private matters. (67)

Highly Offensive Publicity

Under Rhode Island law, to be an actionable invasion of privacy the unreasonable publicity given to a person's private life must be offensive or objectionable to a reasonable person of ordinary sensibilities. (68)

To determine the offensiveness of disclosure, the courts generally consider the customs of the times and the place where the alleged invasion occurred, the occupation of the plaintiff, and the habits of neighbors and members of the community at large. (69)

However, a person "must expect more or less casual observation by his or her neighbors" of ordinary daily activities and that these comings and goings could be described in the media as a matter of casual interest to others. (70)

Matters of Legitimate Public Concern (Newsworthiness)

It has long been recognized that the public has a proper interest in learning more about a number of matters. (71) For example, they include police raids, arrests, marriages and fires, events that by their very nature are newsworthy. (72)

There also are persons who, either voluntarily or involuntarily, become public figures and become part of the day's news.

41

A voluntary public figure is one who engages in public activities, assumes a prominent role in institutions or activities of interest to the public or submits himself or herself or his or her work for public judgment. (73) According to the *Restatement,* "Such a person cannot complain when he or she is given publicity, even though it is not necessarily favorable." (74)

There are other individuals who have not sought publicity nor consented to it, but "through their conduct involuntarily have become a legitimate subject of public interest." (75) For instance, those who commit crimes or are accused of a crime become persons of public interest. So do victims of crime or persons present when a crime is committed or an accident occurs. (76)

Publicity concerning voluntary or involuntary public figures is not limited to the particular events of interest to the public. That interest may extend to some reasonable degree to further information about the person. (77) This means that the life history of a person accused of murder, including private facts about the kind of person he or she may be, is a matter of legitimate public interest. Or the home life and daily habits of a movie actress may be of legitimate and reasonable interest to the public that sees her on screen. Details of an intimate nature, such as her sexual relations, would be considered private. (78)

But when the publicity ceases to be that of informing the public and becomes "a morbid and sensational prying into private lives for its own sake," there is no legitimate news-worthiness of the matter or matters. (79)

The legitimate public interest in a person who either voluntarily or involuntarily becomes a public figure also may include family members. (80)

Newsworthiness Over Time

Generally, even after a number of years, past newsworthy events and the activities of a public figure, including information from old records, may be of legitimate interest to the public. (81)

False Light

Under Rhode Island law, publicity placing a person in a false light occurs when:

(a) there has been some publication of a false or fictitious fact which implies an association which does not exist, even though no one benefits from the disclosure. (82)
(b) such a published or implied association must be objectionable to an ordinary person. (83)
(c) the fact which was disclosed need not be of any benefit to the discloser. (84)

In addition, the *Restatement* requires for false light liability that the defendant have had "knowledge of or acted in reckless disregard as to the falsity of the publicized matter and the false light in which the other would be placed." (85)

False Light and Defamation

In many cases involving a false light invasion, the plaintiff also will sue for libel or slander. (86) Federal courts have frequently noted the similarities between false light and defamation and have incorporated elements of state defamation law in considering false light invasion cases. (87)

However, it is not necessary for a plaintiff to be defamed to bring an action for privacy invasion. "It is enough that he (or she) is given unreasonable and highly objectionable publicity that attributes to him (or her) characteristics, conduct or beliefs that are false and so is placed before the public in a false position." (88)

In Fudge et al v. Penthouse International, Ltd., (89) the plaintiffs were several Rhode Island schoolgirls, who claimed *Penthouse* magazine had placed them in a false light and libeled them when it published a photograph of them giving the

43

"thumbs up sign" to show their disapproval of their school principal, who had segregated them from the boys at recess because of conflicts between the two groups. Over the photo was the headline, "Little Amazons Attack Boys." The plaintiffs alleged the term "amazon" was libelous and that the article and photo presented them in a false light. (90)

The First Circuit Court of Appeals affirmed the federal district court's ruling that the term "amazon" in the headline was a constitutionally protected statement of opinion, adding that it was "no more than rhetorical hyperbole." (91) Thus, it did not meet the "false or fictitious fact" requirement of the state privacy statute. (92)

The court also agreed with the lower court's dismissal of the false light claim for the article and the photograph. However, the appeals court said it "was hampered by the lack of any precedent" concerning the state's "false light" statute, so it looked to the rulings in past libel cases in Rhode Island (93) which said it was for the court to decide "whether a statement is capable of bearing a defamatory meaning." (94) The court said:

> We think it likely that the Rhode Island courts would apply a similar rule in the false light context: the court should make the threshold determination of whether a statement is capable of implying the objectionable association of which the plaintiff (Fudge) complains. (95)

Objectionable to a Reasonable Person

On the second requirement of the state's false light statute, the appeals court said that the photograph and the article, which the girls said implied they were masculine in nature and wanted to dominate the boys, did not imply any association between the girls and the magazine and an endorsement by them of *Penthouse's* views. (96) The court added, "Even if these allegations did involve 'associations' within the meaning of the statute, we would conclude as a matter of law that these associations would not `be objectionable to the ordinary reasonable man under the circumstances'." (97)

Consent

The article about the schoolgirls and the accompanying photograph were in a column in *Penthouse* that was clearly labeled "a compendium" of items "culled from the nation's press." Since the information had come from a third party and not from the plaintiffs, the court said it was "not reasonably capable of implying either the girls' consent to use the photograph and narrative or the girls' endorsement of the magazine's editorial views so as to support (a) statutory false light claim under Rhode Island law." (98)

The Emotional Distress Claim

The tort of intentional infliction of emotional distress continues to be shaped by the state's courts. In the Penthouse decision, the federal appeals court said the plaintiffs had failed to state an emotional distress claim. (99) The court went on to say that the Rhode Island Supreme Court, "in developing the law governing claims for intentional infliction of emotional distress, has relied heavily on the principles" stated in the *Restatement (Second) of Torts:* (100)

> It is for the court to determine, in the first instance, whether the defendant's conduct may reasonably be regarded as so extreme and outrageous as to permit recovery, or whether it is necessarily so. Where reasonable men may differ, it is for the jury, subject to the control of the court, to determine whether, in the particular case, the conduct has been sufficiently extreme and outrageous to result in liability. (101)

In Penthouse, the plaintiffs claimed that the magazine knew or should have known that the publication of their photograph in a sexually explicit men's magazine would "offend, embarrass, shock and outrage" them and their parents. (102) In ruling against the plaintiffs, the court said that there was nothing "false, misleading, suggestive, or inherently offensive or shocking about the photograph itself; plaintiffs merely object to the material that appeared in the neighboring pages." (103) It also said, "Magazines such as *Penthouse* are sufficiently a part of the contemporary scene that their reprinting of relatively innocuous news items or photographs that have already appeared in other media simply cannot be characterized as exceeding all possible bounds of decency, atrocious, or utterly intolerable in a civilized society." (104)

Personal Right to Privacy

Except for the appropriation of a person's name or likeness, an action for invasion of privacy can be maintained only by the person whose privacy supposedly has been invaded. (105)

This means that if a person dies, members of his or her family, for example, cannot maintain an action for invasion of privacy unless their privacy has been invaded along with that of the deceased. (106)

Generally a corporation, a partnership or an unincorporated association has no personal right of privacy and has no cause of action under any of the four areas of invasion of privacy. (107)

Endnotes

1. "The Right of Privacy," 4 Harv. L. Rev. 193 (1890).

2. Mendonsa v. Time Inc., 678 F. Supp. 967 (DRI 1988) citing "The Right to Privacy."

3. Restatement of the Law, 2d, Torts, St. Paul, Minn.: American Law Institute, 1977. (Hereinafter cited as Restatement.)

4. R.I. Gen. Laws 9 1 28.1.

5. Id.

6. 73 A. 97 (RI 1909).

7. Id at 98.

8. Id at 97.

9. Gravina v. Brunswick Corporation, 338 F. Supp. 5 (DRI 1972).

10. Id.

11. R.I. Gen. Laws 9 1 28.

12. Kalian v. People Acting Through Community Effort, Inc. (PACE), 408 A. 2d 608 (RI 1979).

13. Id at 609.

14. Id at 610.

15. Id at 609.

16. R.I. Gen. Laws 9 1 28.1 (a) (1).

17. Restatement 625B.

18. R.I. Gen. Laws 9 1 28.1 (a) (1) (A) (i).

19. Id. at (A) (ii).

20. Id at (B).

21. Restatement 652B at Comment c.

22. Id.

23. In Stessman v. American Black Hawk Broadcasting Co. (416 N.W. 2d 685, 1987), the Iowa Supreme Court said that diners have a right to be free from intrusion, and in Dempsey v. National Enquirer, Inc. (702 F. Supp. 927, 1988), the federal court in Maine said that restaurants are open to the public and there was no intrusion by the media.

24. 890 F.2d 488 (1st Cir. 1989); cert. denied, 110 S. Ct 3269 (1990).

25. Restatement 652B at Comment b.

26. Id.

27. Id. at Comment c.

28. Jane Doe v. Edward A. Sherman Publishing Company, 593 A.2d 457 (RI 1991).

29. Restatement 652B at Comment b.

30. Clift v. Narragansett Television, 688 A. 2d 805 (1996).

31. Id. at 814 citing 73 A. 97.

32. Id. at 814.

33. R.I. Gen. Laws 9 1 28.1 (a) (1) (A) (ii).

34. Restatement 652B at Comment d.

35. Id.

36. Mendonsa v. Time, Inc., 678 F. Supp. 969 (DRI 1988).

37. R.I. Gen. Laws 9 1 28.1 (a) (2) (A)(i,ii).

38. 678 F. Supp. 973.

39. R.I. Gen. Laws 9 1 28.

40. 678 F. Supp. 973.

41. R.I. Gen. Laws 9 1 28.

42. Id.

43. Id.

44. 678 F. Supp. 967.

45. Id. at 968.

46. Id. at 973.

47. Id.

48. Id. at 972.

49. Id. at 971 citing Gautier v. Pro Football, Inc., 107 N.E.2d 485 (1952)

50. Id. at 971.

51. Id. at 972, citing 107 N.E.2d at 488.

52. Id. at 972, citing Blumenthal v. Picture Classics, 235 A.D. 570 (1932).

53. R.I. Gen. Laws 9 1 28.

54. R.I. Gen. Laws 9 1 28.1 (b).

55. R.I. Gen. Laws 9 1 28.1 (a) (4).

56. Id. at (a) (4) (A) (i).

57. Id. at (a) (4) (A) (ii).

58. Id. at (a) (4) (B).

59. Restatement 652D at Comment a.

60. Id.

61. Id.

62. 652D at Comment b.

63. R.I. Gen. Laws 9 1 28.1 (c).

64. 593 A.2d 458 (RI 1991).

65. Id.

66. Restatement 652D at Comment b.

67. Id.

68. R.I. Gen. Laws 9 1 28.1 (a) (3) (A) (ii).

69. Restatement 652D at Comment c.

70. Id.

71. Id. at Comment d.

72. Id. at Comment g.

73. Id. at Comment e.

74. Id.

75. Id. at Comment f.

76. Id.

77. Id. at Comment h.

78. Id.

79. Id.

80. Id. at Comment i.

81. Id. at Comment k.

82. R.I. Gen. Laws 9 1 28.1 (a)(4) (i)

83. Id. at (ii)

84. Id. at (a) (4) (B)

85. Restatement 652E.

86. Id. at Comment b.

87. Leslie Fudge et al. v. Penthouse International, Ltd., 840 F.2d 1018 (1st Cir. 1988) citing Braun v. Flynt 726 F.2d 245, 250, 252, (5th Cir.1984).

88. Restatement 652E at Comment b.

89. 840 F.2d 1012.

90. Id. at 1014.

91. Id. at 1016.

92. Id. at 1018.

93. Id. citing Healey v. New England Newspapers, Inc., 520 A.2d 147, 150 (R.I. 1987) (citing Restatement [Second] of Torts, Section 614) and Reid v. Providence Journal Co., 37 A. 637 (1897).

94. Id. at 1018, citing 520 A. 2d 147.

95. Id. at 1018.

96. Id. at 1019.

97. Id.

98. Id. at 1013.

99. 840 F.2d 1020, 1021.

100. Id.

101. Id. citing Restatement 46 at Comment h.

102. 840 F. 2d 1020.

103. Id. at 1021.

104. Id. In Clift v. Narragansett Television, 688 A.2d 805 (1996), the R.I. Supreme Court determined the plaintiff had failed "to state a viable claim for the intentional infliction of emotional distress."

105. Restatement at 652I.

106. Id. at Comment a.

107. Id. at Comment c.

Obscenity Law in Rhode Island

Rhode Island's obscenity law (1) is based on the standards set forth by the United States Supreme Court in Miller v. California in 1973. (2)

To determine whether a publication, a movie, a "performance" or "other material" is obscene, the Rhode Island law says the materials must be "taken as a whole," (3) and the following criteria must be met:

- "the average person, applying contemporary community standards would find that the work...appeals to the prurient interest";
- "the work depicts or describes, in a patently offensive way, sexual conduct";
- "the work...lacks serious literary, artistic, political or scientific value." (4)

The law defines some of the words used in the above criteria:

> "Performance" means any play, motion picture, dance or other exhibition performed before an audience. "Material" means anything tangible that can be used or "adapted" to arouse prurient interest through reading or observation. "Community standards" means the whole state; "patently offensive" means the material is so offensive on its face that it affronts the "current standards of decency," which are those of the community, that is, Rhode Island. (5)

"Sexual conduct" means:

> ... an act of intercourse, normal or perverted" actual or simulated including genital genital, anal genital, or oral genital intercourse, whether between human beings or between a human being and an animal;

> sado masochistic abuse, meaning flagellation or torture by or upon a person in an act of apparent sexual stimulation or gratification; masturbation, excretory functions and lewd exhibitions of the genitals. (6)

Distribution and Sales of Obscenity

The Rhode Island obscenity law makes it illegal for anyone to "willfully or knowingly" promote obscene materials for commercial gain in the state. Punishment is a fine of no less than $100 and no more than $1,000 or imprisonment for not more than two years or both a fine and imprisonment. (7)

Included in the definition of "promote" is manufacturing, selling, lending or giving, mailing, exhibiting or advertising obscene materials. "Knowingly" means "having knowledge of the character and content of the material or failure on notice to exercise reasonable inspection which would disclose the content and character" of the obscene materials. (8)

It also is illegal for a person, a corporation or an association to make the receipt of obscene materials, such as books and magazines, a condition to delivery of non obscene publications. (9)

Obscene Materials and Minors

Under Rhode Island law, anyone who is found guilty of "willfully or knowingly" selling or exhibiting obscene materials to minors—those under the age of 18—is subject to a fine of not less than $100 and no more than $1,000 or imprisonment for not more than two years or both. (10)

"Knowingly" is defined as "having knowledge of the character and content of the publication or failure on notice to exercise reasonable inspection which would disclose the content and character of (the publication)." (11)

The law also applies to a person who lends, gives away or advertises obscene materials to minors or has in his or her possession obscene materials with the intent of selling or distributing them to minors. This includes displaying such materials at newsstands or in any business establishment frequented by minors. (12)

The "materials" can be movies, photographs, books or magazines of which the cover or the content consists of or is predominantly made up of explicit representations of 'sexual conduct,' or 'sexual excitement' or 'nudity' and which is indecent for minors." (13)

"Indecent for minors" means that the material "(a) appeals to the prurient interest in sex of minors, and (b) is patently offensive to prevailing standards in the adult community with respect to what is suitable material for minors, and (c) lacks serious literary, artistic, political or scientific value for minors." (14)

"Sexual excitement" is defined as meaning the "human genitals in a state of sexual stimulation or arousal." "Sexual conduct" refers to the "act of human masturbation, sexual intercourse, sodomy, fondling, or other erotic touching of human genitals, pubic region, buttock or female breasts." (15)

The law defines "nudity" as those parts of the body—human genitals, pubic regions, buttock and the female breasts "below a point immediately above the top of the areola" as "less than completely and opaquely covered." (16)

Minors in Rhode Island also are protected by law from being used in a publication or a movie in a setting "which taken as a whole suggests to the average person that such child has engaged in, or is about to engage in any sexual act..." (17) A person convicted for a first offense under the law can be imprisoned up to 10 years or fined not more than $10,000 or both. Subsequent convictions could mean imprisonment up to 15 years or a fine of up not more than $15,000 or both. (18)

Judicial Procedures

Rhode Island has a series of statutes spelling out the adjudication process for obscene publications. (19)

Briefly, if the attorney general has reasonable cause to believe that a person is selling, distributing or exhibiting obscene materials, such as books, magazines and movies (20), he or she may file a petition asking the court to determine if the material is obscene. (21) This could result in the court:
- dismissing the petition if it finds no probable cause to believe the material is obscene. (22)
- issuing a notice for a hearing on the alleged obscene materials within 30 days (the notice must be published once a week for two successive weeks in a local, general circulation newspaper). (23)
- or issuing a temporary restraining order against the sale, distribution of exhibition of the materials alleged to be obscene. (24)

If a temporary restraining order is issued, a hearing must be held within one day, and the court must render a decision within 48 hours after the hearing. Otherwise, the order expires. (25) While a restraining order is in effect, anyone who sells, distributes or exhibits or even has possession of the alleged obscene materials "is presumed to have knowledge that (the materials are) obscene." (26)

Local Licensing

Rhode Island law stipulates that the licensing of amusements, including movies, exhibitions and performances, is the province of the cities and towns. Specifically, a town council, a board of police commissioners or other licensing board or authority may require a license for a place within the community where the shows or exhibits are presented. (27) The word "obscene" does not appear in the statute. However, the state Supreme Court has handed down decisions in several obscenity cases in recent years that cite the authority of local licensing boards to determine whether a movie is obscene within the parameters of the state's obscenity law. (28)

Verbal Obscenity

In Rhode Island it is unlawful for a person to use "threatening, vulgar, indecent, obscene or immoral language" over the telephone. Punishment is a fine of not more than $500 or imprisonment for not more than one year or both. (29) Prosecution takes place in the jurisdiction either where the call was made or where it was received. (30)

Endnotes

1. R.I. Gen. Laws 11 31 1.

2. Miller v. California, 93 S.Ct. 2607 (1973).

3. R.I. Gen. Laws 11 31 1.

4. Id.

5. Id.

6. Id.

7. Id.

8. Id.

9. R.I. Gen. Laws 11 31 12.

10. R.I. Gen. Laws 11 31 10.

11. Id.

12. Id.

13. Id.

14. Id.

15. Id.

16. Id.

17. R.I. Gen. Laws 11 9 1.1.

18. Id.

19. R.I. Gen. Laws, Chapt. 27, Sections 12 27 1 through 12 27 12.

20. R.I. Gen. Laws 12 27 1.

21. R.I. Gen. Laws 12 27 2.

22. R.I. Gen. Laws 12 27 3.

23. Id.

24. R.I. Gen. Laws 12 27 4

25. Id.

26. R.I. Gen. Laws 12 27 10.

27. R.I. Gen. Laws 5 22 5.

28. For instance, the Rhode Island Supreme Court ruled in State v. Berberian (427 A. 2d 1298 (1981)) that the defendant had the right to rely on a license to show films issued by the Providence Bureau of Licenses, thereby barring any criminal prosecution under the state's obscenity statute. The court said "it is clear that the Legislature has delegated to the Bureau the responsibility of regulating the exhibition of films pursuant to (Gen. Laws) 5 22 5."

29. R.I. Gen. Laws 11 35 7.

30. R.I. Gen. Laws 11 35 19.

The Regulation of Advertising in Rhode Island

The United States Supreme Court has handed down a number of decisions in recent years that extend some constitutional protections to commercial advertising. In the 1980 decision of Central Hudson Gas & Electric v. Public Service Commission, the court set forth a four part test to govern the regulation of advertising. (1)

First, it must be determined if the advertising is eligible for First Amendment protection; second, the advertising must promote a legal product or service and cannot be deceptive, misleading or false; third, the government must demonstrate that any regulation placed on the advertising must advance the government's interest, and fourth, that regulation must be only as broad as necessary to advance the government's interest. (2)

In addition, the Rhode Island General Assembly has developed a body of law that regulates advertising, including professional services, businesses and products, political advertising, and outdoor advertising. (3)

Deceptive Advertising in Rhode Island

The Deceptive Trade Practices law (4) includes a number of general regulations of advertising in the state. For instance, it is illegal to advertise goods if the intent is not to sell them as advertised. (5) It is illegal to advertise goods or services if the supply is not sufficient to meet the demand, unless the advertisement states that the quantity is limited. (6) Making false or misleading statements of fact concerning the reasons for the existence of, or amounts of, price reductions is a deceptive trade practice. (7)

Advertising any brand name goods for sale and then selling substituted brand names in their place is illegal (8) as is failure to include the brand name and/or manufacturer of goods for sale in an advertisement. (9) If goods are used or second-hand, that information must be stated in the advertisement. (10) If claims of safety, performance and comparative price are included in an advertisement, the information substantiating the claim must be made available if requested by "any person, the consumer council or the attorney general." (11)

The attorney general may seek an injunction to restrain a person from engaging in alleged deceptive advertising. (12)

A separate law makes it a criminal offense for a "person, firm, corporation or association" to use false or deceptive statements in advertisements, in print or broadcast, regarding merchandise, securities or services. (13) The penalty is either a fine or not less than $50 and not more than $500 or imprisonment for not more than 90 days or both a fine and imprisonment. (14)

Immunity of the Media

Radio or television stations or the publishers of newspapers, magazines or "any other recognized advertising media or printer" are exempt from prosecution if they publish or broadcast an advertisement "without actual knowledge of its falsity." (15)

Professional Services

State laws forbid deceptive advertising for a number of professional services, such as those of podiatrists, (16) chiropodists, (17) optometrists and opticians, (18) brokers and investors, (19) and lawyers (20). For example, lawyers can advertise, but by law they are not permitted "to advertise contrary to the ethics of their profession." (21)

The rules of the Rhode Island Supreme Court define the parameters of advertising by members of the bar. (22) Lawyers can not make false or misleading communications about their services. (23) They can advertise their services through the public media, such as a telephone directory, a legal directory, a newspaper or other periodical, outdoor advertising, radio or television. (24) They must keep a copy or recording of the advertisement for two years after it last was printed or broadcast along with a record of when and where it was used. (25)

Physicians and surgeons, like lawyers, can advertise but not if the advertisement "is intended or has a tendency to deceive the public." (26) Another law which regulates physicians and surgeons and which has drawn criticism from the medical community mandates that if a medical review board finds a physician or surgeon guilty of professional misconduct that information must be made public. (27)

Regulation of Products and Businesses

Under Rhode Island law, the advertising of more than 25 different types of products and businesses is regulated. For instance, barbers, (28) hairdressers, cosmeticians and manicurists, (29) and anyone performing electrolysis (30) are forbidden from using deceptive advertising. It is unlawful for health maintenance organizations (HMOs) to advertise their coverage in a false or misleading manner. (31) Vendors can not advertise until they have been issued a license by the state, or the city or town. (32)

Detectives must cease all advertising if the local licensing authority rules that the advertising tends to mislead the public.

They can lose their licenses if they continue to advertise. (33) Travel agencies, too, can have their licenses revoked if they use "intentionally misleading advertising." (34)

Under the state's motor vehicle laws, a licensed wrecker, after giving notice to the registered owner of a towed motor vehicle to be sold, must advertise the sale for two consecutive days for at least 10 days and no more than 14 days before the sale. The notice must appear in a daily newspaper of general circulation. (35) Businesses which sell or lease used and new motor vehicles are prohibited from using false or misleading advertising. (36)

Real estate brokers or salespersons can have their licenses revoked or suspended if they make any misleading or untruthful advertising. (37)

Newspapers and other periodicals can be found guilty of a misdemeanor and be fined up to $1,000 if they misrepresent their circulation for the purpose of securing advertisements. (38)

The advertising of a variety of products is regulated by state statutes. For instance, advertisements for imported goods for sale must contain the words "Imported Goods" in letters at least as large as the figures indicating the price, and if no price is listed, then the letters must be as large as the body type of the advertisement. (39) It also is unlawful to advertise goods being offered for sale at below the regular price unless the regular price is posted as the point of purchase. (40)

Until 1996, Rhode Island forbade a liquou licensee to advertise any reference to prices of liquor offered for sale in the state. (41) The law applied to newspapers, periodicals, radio or television broadcasters and other persons or businesses in the state which sold or were in the business of advertising alcoholic beverages. (42) The Rhode Island Supreme Courthad upheld the statute in two separate cases in 1985. (43) Then in 1996 the U.S. Supreme court overturned the ban saying it "abridged speech in violation of the First Amendment.". (44)

A statute makes it unlawful to advertise foods, drugs and cosmetics in a false or misleading manner. (45) Advertisements for consumer goods sold primarily in grocery stores, such as food, beverages and everyday household items, must state the unit price along with the total price. (46) There are laws that make it illegal to make false representations and statements about the rates and terms for educational loans, (47) for loans for mortgages, (48) and for loans under $5,000. (49)

Only farm products, eggs and poultry produced in Rhode Island can be advertised as "native" or "native grown." (50)

When cigarettes without the required stamp tax are seized by the government as contraband, the government, after a court hearing, may advertise the cigarettes for sale, for at least five days, in a newspaper published and circulated in the town where the seizure took place. (51)

Anyone who uses a fax machine to transmit unsolicited advertisements for "the sale of any real property, goods or services" can be fined up to $200 for each occurrence. (52)

Political Advertising

All advertising in newspapers or other periodicals designed to "aid, injure or defeat any candidate for public office" must include the name of the chairperson or secretary or the name of two of the officers of the organization submitting the advertisement. The name of some voter who is responsible for the advertisement along with his or her address is also acceptable. If the advertisement is inserted in the "reading columns" of the newspaper or periodical, it must carry the word "advertisement" in a separate type not smaller than that of the body type of the newspaper or periodical. (53) Posters, flyers and circulars used as political advertising also must be signed by those mentioned above. (54) Violation of these laws constitutes a misdemeanor. (55)

Newspapers, periodicals, radio and television can charge for a political advertisement a sum no greater than what they would charge if the advertisement were not political. If convicted, the medium would receive a civil penalty of $500. (56)

Elected officials in Rhode Island are not allowed by law to spend public funds for "any publication, advertisement, broadcast or telecast of his or her photograph, voice or other likeness" which would be broadcast or distributed to the public during the 120 days preceding a primary or general election in which the person is a candidate. (57) However, the elected official may appear on regular programming operated by the General Assembly or on television stations operated by the Rhode Island public telecommunications authority. (58)

Outdoor Advertising

Rhode Island has laws that regulate the display of outdoor advertising. The erection and maintenance of outdoor advertising adjacent to interstate, primary and secondary road systems in the state are regulated by the director of transportation. (59) Signs adjacent to interstate and primary highway systems also are regulated by the Federal Highway Beautification Act of 1958. (60) Any outdoor advertising that distracts the operators of motor vehicles and interferes with traffic signals and signs is considered "a public nuisance." (61)

State law limits outdoor advertising to the following:

(a) directional and other official signs and notices that are authorized by a public agency or body.

(b) signs, displays and devices that advertise the sale or lease of property upon which they are located.

(c) signs, displays and devices advertising activities conducted on the property upon which they are located, assuming they conform to federal law and certain rules of the state Department of Transportation.

(d) no more than one two sided sign at bus shelters erected by the state Department of Transportation or the Rhode Island Public Transit Authority.

(e) lawfully permitted signs, displays and devices already in existence that may be relocated to other permitted locations with the approval of the appropriate government agency, provided the relocated sign remains the same or smaller and conforms to local zoning requirements. (62)

Also maps and informational directories and advertising pamphlets can be made available at safety rest areas along highways. (63)

Cities and towns have the authority to regulate outdoor advertising in their municipalities as to the place where the advertising may be permitted, the size and kind of structures upon which the advertising may be placed, and the subject matter that can appear on the structures, "provided, those regulations shall be reasonable in their requirements." (64)

Discrimination in Advertising

It is illegal for the owner or the agent of the owner of any housing to "issue an advertisement relating to the sale, rental or lease" of such housing which discriminates on the basis of race, color, religion, sex, marital status, country of ancestral origin, handicap, age of familial status. (65) Likewise, it is unlawful for an employer to print or cause to be printed or published any notice or advertisement that discriminates on the basis of those same areas. (66)

Legal Notice Requirements

Requirements for legal notices and advertisements are scattered throughout the state statutes. Many are a part of the laws governing aspects of cities and towns. For instance, if a city of town wants to establish an official map (67) or make changes in its existing map (68), it must give at least 10 days' notice of the hearing in a newspaper of general circulation published in the city or town. (69)

Notice of a public hearing on the adoption, repeal or amendment of a zoning ordinance in a city or town must be given in the form of a notice to be published in a newspaper of general circulation within the city or town at least once each week for three successive weeks prior to the hearing. The notice must be "published as display advertising, using a type size at least as large as the normal type size used by the newspaper in its news articles." (70) The information must include the date, time, and details of the proposed change. (71)

In probate cases where a notice is required, the notice must be given in the form of an advertisement for 14 days, once a week at least, in a newspaper that circulates in the city or town where the probate matter is to be acted upon. (72) A separate statute allows the notice to be published in a foreign language newspaper circulated in the city or town. (73)

Some of the other state and local matters that must be announced to the public in the form of a printed notice include city and town budgets (74), violations of the state building code (75), rate changes by public utilities (76), and the sale of mortgages and deeds of trust. (77)

Regulation of Newspaper Boxes

In 1987, the federal court in Rhode Island found unconstitutional a Newport city ordinance banning the placement of coin operated newspaper vending machines on public rights of way. (78) The court said the ordinance "failed to advance the city's aesthetic interest," and it was "not narrowly tailored to further the city's interest in facilitating the flow of pedestrian traffic on sidewalks." The fact that the newspapers were available at private outlets, the court noted, did not authorize the city to ban their sale on public streets and sidewalks. (79)

Miscellaneous Notes

It is a false, deceptive or misleading advertising practice if a person, firm or corporation prints, publishes or circulates literature or advertising material used in connection with "any promotion or advertising scheme," (80) such as a retail establishment offering gifts or prizes as part of a contest. (81)

In Rhode Island anyone who "willfully" sends a fraudulent birth, marriage or death notice to a newspaper can be fined up to $100. (82)

As mentioned in earlier chapters, it is illegal in Rhode Island to advertise obscene materials. (83) And under the state's privacy laws, it is illegal to use a person's name, portrait or photograph for advertising purposes without the person's written consent. (84)

In 1989, a convicted child molester was ordered by a Rhode Island Superior Court judge to purchase an advertisement in The Providence Journal Bulletin to inform the public of his conviction. The ad carried the man's photo and a caption in which he urged other child molesters to seek professional help. (85)

Endnotes

1. 447 U.S. 557 (1980).

2. Id.

3. see following citations.

4. R.I. Gen. Laws 6 13.1 1.

5. Id. at section I.

6. Id. at section J.

7. Id. at section K.

8. Id. at section O.

9. Id. at section P.

10. Id.

11. Id. at section Q.

12. R.I. Gen. Laws 6 13.1 7.

13. R.I. Gen. Laws 11 18 10.

14. R.I. Gen. Laws 11 18 12.

15. R.I. Gen. Laws 11 18 11.

16. R.I. Gen. Laws 5 29 25.

17. Id.

18. R.I. Gen. Laws 5 35 20, section b.

19. R.I. Gen. Laws 7 11 14, 17 11 101, section 9. Laws involving the sale and advertising of securities have been undergoing extensive revision by the General Assembly. Under R.I. Gen. Law 7 11 16, the state director of business regulation must notify newspapers receiving and printing advertisements of securities that the privilege of selling those securities has been cancelled. Any newspaper that continues to publish the ads will be in violation of the law.

20. R.I. Gen. Laws 11 27 10.

21. Id.

22. Rules of professional conduct, Supreme Court, Rule 47.

23. Id. at section 7.1.

24. Id. at section 7.2 (a).

25. Id. at (b).

26. R.I. Gen. Laws 5 37 5.1.

27. R.I. Gen. Law 5 37 5.2.

28. R.I. Gen. Laws 5 27 18.

29. R.I. Gen. Laws 5 10 21.

30. R.I. Gen. Laws 5 32 10.

31. R.I. Gen. Laws 27 41 14.

32. R.I. Gen. Laws 5 15 11.

33. R.I. Gen. Laws 5 5 17.

34. R.I. Gen. Laws 5 52 7.

35. R.I. Gen. Laws 31 22 18.

36. R.I. Gen. Laws 31 5.1 4.

37. R.I. Gen. Laws 5 20.5 14.

38. R.I. Gen. Laws 11 18 5.

39. R.I. Gen. Laws 5 41 2.

40. R.I. Gen. Laws 6 13 11.

41. R.I. Gen. Laws 3 8 8.1.

42. Id.

43. S & S Liquor Mart v. Pastore, 497 A.2d 729 (R.I. 1985).

44. 497 A.2d 334.

45. R.I. Gen. Laws 21 31 19. Also, see R.I. Gen. Law 21 9 12 for advertising prohibitions of frozen desserts and/or frozen dessert mixes.

46. R.I. Gen. Laws 6 31 4.

47. R.I. Gen. Laws 19 25.1 27.

48. R.I. Gen. Laws 19 25.4 20.

49. R.I. Gen. Laws 19 25 20.

50. R.I. Gen. Laws 21 32 1.

51. R.I. Gen. Laws 44 20 38.

52. R.I. Gen. Laws 11 35 27.

53. R.I. Gen. Laws 17 23 1.

54. R.I. Gen. Laws 17 23 2.

55. R.I. Gen. Laws 17 23 3.

56. R.I. Gen. Laws 17 23 14.

57. R.I. Gen. Laws 17 23 18.

58. Id.

59. R.I. Gen. Laws 24 10.1 1.

60. Title 23, U.S. Code, Highways.

61. R.I. Gen. Laws 24 10.1 1.

62. R.I. Gen. Laws 24 10.1 3.

63. R.I. Gen. Laws 25 10.1 10.

64. R.I. Gen. Laws 5 18 2.

65. R.I. Gen. Laws 34 37 4.

66. R.I. Gen. Laws 28 5 7.

67. R.I. Gen. Laws 45 23.1 1.

68. R.I. Gen. Laws 45 32.1 2.

69. R.I. Gen. Laws 45 23.1 1.

70. R.I. Gen. Laws 45 24 53.

71. Id.

72. R.I. Gen. Laws 33 22 11.

73. R.I. Gen. Laws 33 22 13.

74. R.I. Gen. Laws 44 35 8.

75. R.I. Gen. Laws 23 27.3 122.1.

76. R.I. Gen. Laws 39 3 11.

77. R.I. Gen. Laws 34 27 4. In 1981, the R.I. Supreme Court ruled in Beaufort v. Warwick Credit Union (437 A.2d 1375) that a newspaper circulated six days a week, excluding Sundays and holidays, was a "daily newspaper" within the requirements of 34 27 4 that notice of a foreclosure sale be published in a daily newspaper at least once a week for three successive weeks before the sale.

78. Providence Journal Company , et al v. City of Newport, 665 F. Supp. 107 (DCRI 1987).

79. Id.

80. R.I. Gen. Laws 11 50 6.

81. R.I. Gen. Laws 11 50 1.

82. R.I. Gen. Laws 11 18 3.

83. R.I. Gen. Laws 11 31 1.

84. R.I. Gen. Laws 9 1 28.

85. "Convicted molester obeys order, buys ad urging others to seek help," The Providence Journal Bulletin, Nov. 11, 1989.

Rhode Island's Newsperson's Privilege

The civil rights movement and the war protests of the late 1960s and early 1970s induced journalists to occasionally rely on confidential sources to report the news. Eventually some of these journalists were summoned before grand juries and asked to reveal their sources.

In 1972, the United States Supreme Court ruled that reporters do not have a First Amendment privilege to refuse to reveal confidential sources and information. Speaking for the court, Justice Byron White wrote that the court was being "asked to create another (privilege) by interpreting the First Amendment to grant newsmen a testimonial privilege that other citizens do not enjoy. This we decline to do." (1)

However, the court left it open for state legislatures to pass laws protecting journalists and their sources. And many did.

The Rhode Island newsperson's privilege law* was adopted in 1971, just prior to the Branzburg ruling. (2) It was first tested in 1984 in a federal court. (3) Then in the early 1990s, the Rhode Island Supreme Court looked to Branzburg in interpreting some parts of the law in two separate cases. (4)

The state court said that its reading of Branzburg, along with Herbert v. Lando, (5) "leads us to the conclusion that the

---

* The correct name of the law in The Newsman's Privilege Act. However, the itent of this book is to be gender neutral whenever possible.

Supreme Court of the United States has rejected the proposition that there is a First Amendment privilege accorded to newspersons to refuse to disclose information, confidential or otherwise, which is necessary to a litigated case." (6)

The court noted that some of the lower federal courts have relied on Justice Lewis Powell's concurring opinion in Branzburg to create a qualified privilege. "We believe this reliance is misplaced," the court said. (7)

The State Statute

Who Is Protected

The law protects a wide variety of individuals working in the mass media. They are reporters, editors, commentators, journalists, writers, correspondents, news photographers or "other person(s) directly engaged in the gathering or presenting of news for any accredited newspaper, periodical, press association, newspaper syndicate, wire service, or radio or television station." (8) A newspaper or periodical must be issued at regular intervals and have a paid circulation. (9)

The law does not appear to protect public relations practitioners, freelance writers who are working without authorization from a news outlet, book authors, and academic researchers. (10)

Publication

Although the law says that a journalist is protected "in the gathering or presenting of news," (11) the Rhode Island Supreme Court in Outlet Communications, Inc. v. State of Rhode Island said that the unpublished portions of a television interview conducted on a public sidewalk at the request of a person who was wanted by the authorities in connection with an ongoing grand jury investigation were not protected by the privilege law. (12)

Confidentiality and Protection

The law protects journalists from revealing a confidential association, confidential information and the source of any confidential information. (13) In Outlet v. State, the state supreme court said "information must be given in secret or in confidence to the news entity that claims the privilege in order to acquire the protection of confidentiality." (14) But the court went on to say that because the reporter from the Outlet's television station, Channel 10, interviewed the source in a public place, "the acquisition of the information was anything but secret or confidential." (15)

Legal Forums

The privilege can be asserted in any court, before a grand jury, an agency, department or commission of the state. (16)

Privilege Waiver

The federal district court said that the journalist in the Fischer v. McGowan case did not waive his privilege under the Rhode Island law when he disclosed some sources in an allegedly defamatory article but not other confidential sources. (17)

In Capuano v. Outlet, a libel case in which a journalist working for the Outlet's television station invoked the newsperson's privilege, the state supreme court said that the journalist by pleading a defense of good faith and further testifying that the allegedly defamatory article was based on reliable confidential sources waived the privilege. (18)

Qualifications

The Rhode Island law states that the privilege does not apply to any information that has "at any time" been published, broadcast or "otherwise made public" by the person claiming the privilege. (19)

The privilege does not apply to the source of any allegedly defamatory information in any case where the defendant, in a civil action for defamation, asserts a defense based on that information. (20)

In Capuano v. Outlet the state's high court ruled that the reporter lost his right to assert a privilege in a libel action when it meant that the plaintiffs would have "to depose scores of individuals" the reporter claimed could have been among his confidential sources. (21)

In that case, the Rhode Island court turned to decisions by the Massachusetts (22) and New Hampshire (23) courts to determine that the reporter had no First Amendment privilege to refuse to divulge confidential information and sources in a defamation action "when this information is obviously both relevant and essential to plaintiffs in sustaining their heavy burden of proof." (24)

In addition, the court said that even though the reporter was not the defendant in the defamation case against the television station, the statutory exclusion regarding defamation applied to the reporter when the station had claimed the privilege. (25)

The privilege also does not apply to the source of any information concerning the details of any grand jury or other proceeding which was required to be secret under state law. (26)

Judicial Procedure

In a case where a journalist has claimed a privilege under the law, the person or agency seeking the information or the source of the information may ask the superior court for an order divesting the privilege. If the court finds that there is "substantial evidence" that disclosure of the privilege is necessary to permit a criminal prosecution for the commission of a specific felony or to prevent a threat to a human life and the source of the information is not available from any prospective witnesses, the court "may make such order as may be proper under the circumstance." (27)

Endnotes

1. Branzburg v. Hayes, 408 U.S. 690 (1972).

2. R.I. Gen. Laws 9 19.1 1 3.

3. Fischer v. McGowan, 585 F. Supp. 978 (DRI 1984).

4. Capuano v. The Outlet Company, 579 A.2d 469 (R.I. 1990) and Outlet Communications, Inc. v. State, 588 A.2d 1050 (R.I. 1991).

5. Herbert v. Lando, 441 U.S. 153 (1979).

6. 579 A.2d at 474.

7. Id.

8. R.I. Gen. Laws 9 19.1 2.

9. R.I. Gen. Laws 9 19.1 1.

10. 9 19.1 2.

11. Id.

12. 588 A.2d at 1051.

13. 9 19.1 2.

14. 588 A.2d at 1052.

15. Id.

16. 9 19.1 2.

17. 585 F. Supp. 978.

18. 579 A.2d at 477.

19. 9 19.1 3 (a).

20. 9 19.1 3 (b) (1).

21. 579 A.2d at 476.

22. In the Matter Roche, 381 Mass. 624 (1980).

23. Downing v. Monitor Publishing Co., 415 A. 2d 683 (1980).

24. 579 A.2d at 476.

25. Id. at 477.

26. 9 19.1 3 (b) (2).

27. 9 19.1 3 (c).

The Media and the Judiciary in Rhode Island

The Sixth Amendment to the United States Constitution and Section 10 of Article I of the Rhode Island Constitution guarantee criminal defendants the right to a speedy and public trial by an impartial jury. As noted earlier in this book, the First Amendment to the U.S. Constitution and Section 20 of Article I of the state's constitution guarantee freedom of the press. Sometimes these two rights conflict when publicity about a criminal case makes it impossible for a defendant to receive a fair trial by an impartial jury.

Courts have remedies available to ensure that prejudicial publicity does not interfere with the individual's right to a fair trial. They include change of venue or shifting the location of a trial; change of venire or changing the jury pool rather than the location of the trial; severance which means that when two persons are charged with the same or related crime, the trials will be held separately; continuance or postponement of a trial until the publicity dies down; or, as a last resort, a new trial. Remedies to ensure an impartial jury are voir dire or the questioning of prospective jurors to detect any biases; the sequestration or locking up the jury, and judicial admonition whereby the judge, instead of sequestering the jury, warns jurors against reading or watching anything about the trial.

In Rhode Island guidelines to ensure a fair trial are found in case decisions, laws enacted by the General Assembly, and in the published rules of the various courts in the state.

Trial Publicity

In its rules governing a fair trial, the Rhode Island Supreme Court acknowledges that "it is difficult to strike a balance between protecting the right to a fair trial and safeguarding the right of free expression." (1) It also states, "Preserving the right to a fair trial necessarily entails some curtailment of the information that may be disseminated about a party prior to trial, particularly whereby trial by jury is involved." (2) Without limits, the result would be "the practical nullification of the protective effect of the rules of forensic decorum and the exclusionary rules of evidence." (3) On the other hand, vital interests of society are served by the free dissemination of information about legal proceedings because "the public has a right to know about the threats to its safety and measures aimed at assuring its security." (4)

According to the Supreme Court Rules, a lawyer can not make public statements outside the courtroom that could prejudice a proceeding, (5) including a civil matter triable to a jury, a criminal matter, or any other proceeding that could result in incarceration. (6)

These prohibited public statements may relate to the character, credibility, reputation or criminal records of a party to a case, a witness, or a suspect in a criminal investigation, or the identity of a witness or the expected testimony of a witness or party to the case. (7) Lawyers involved in a criminal proceeding or one that could lead to incarceration are forbidden, under the court rules, from discussing the possibility of a plea of guilty to an offense or the existence of a confession, admission or statement given by a defendant or suspect or that person's refusal to make a statement. (8) They also may not discuss physical evidence, the results of tests or examinations or the failure of a person to submit to an examination or test. (9)

Lawyers may not publicly give an opinion as to the guilt or innocence of a defendant in a criminal case (10) nor can they discuss information they know or "reasonably should know" is likely to be inadmissible as evidence in a trial or, if disclosed, could create a substantial risk or prejudicing an impartial jury. (11)

What lawyers involved in such cases may discuss are the general nature of the claim or defense (12), information contained in a public record (13), that an investigation is in progress, including the general scope of the investigation, the offense or claim or defense involved, and, except when prohibited by law, the identity of the person involved. (14) Lawyers may discuss the scheduling or result of any litigation (15), the request for assistance in obtaining necessary evidence and information (16), and a warning of danger if there is reason to believe the behavior of a person involved may cause substantial harm to an individual or to the public interests. (17)

In a criminal case, a lawyer also may speak publicly on the identity, residence, occupation and family status of the accused (18), and, if the accused has not been apprehended, the lawyer may release information to the public necessary to help catch the person. (19) The lawyer also may give out the fact, time and place of arrest (20), the identity of the investigating and arresting officers or agencies, and the length of the investigation. (21)

Access to the Court

Official court records, such as testimony of witnesses, opening statements, closing arguments, indictments, complaints, and other materials, have long been open to inspection and copying by the public and the press under common law. However, some areas of a court proceeding can be ordered closed by the trial judge.

In 1985 in State v. Cianci (22), the Rhode Island Supreme Court developed a four part inquiry that a trial court must make before imposing a protective order on any part of the proceeding. (23) The court based the four part inquiry on earlier decisions by the United States Supreme Court which had recognized the public's right of access to many kinds of court proceedings, although under certain circumstances a court can exclude the public. (24)

Closure is justified, the Rhode Island court said, if a protective order meets the following criteria:
- It must be narrowly tailored to serve the interests sought to be protected.
- It must be the only reasonable alternative.
- It must permit access to those parts of the record not deemed sensitive.
- It must be accompanied by the trial justice's specific findings explaining the necessity for the order. (25)

In State v. Cianci, at the request of the state and the defendant, a judge in Superior Court entered a protective order sealing pretrial discovery documents without first holding a hearing. (26) Cianci, the mayor of Providence, had been charged with a variety of crimes, including kidnapping and extortion. (27) The Providence Journal Company and the Outlet Company (Channel 10) then asked the court to set aside the protective order. The court refused. (28) The two news organizations appealed to the state Supreme Court. By this time, Cianci had pleaded nolo contendere to some of the charges, while others were dropped. He had received suspended sentences and probation. As a result, he was forced to resign as mayor. (29)

The Rhode Island Supreme Court said the request by the news organizations for access to the discovery documents was "technically moot" because the criminal case had been settled. (30) It did note that the trial justice "acted well within his discretion in entering the protective order" to seal the documents, but first he should have held a public hearing. (31) In developing the four part inquiry in this decision, the Supreme Court said it was giving "guidance in future cases." (32)

In 1991, the state Supreme Court looked to the four part

inquiry in reviewing a Superior Court judge's decision to close the individual voir dire examination of jurors in a murder case to the press and the public. (33) *The Providence Journal* and its reporter, Tracy Breton, orally protested the closure because it violated their First Amendment right of access to criminal proceedings. (34) They claimed that the trial court failed to show that the closure was necessary to protect the privacy rights of the prospective jurors or the defendant's right to a fair trial. (35)

In applying the four part inquiry in *The Providence Journal* v. Superior Court, the state Supreme Court said, "We come to the conclusion that the trial court's closure...may have been an unconstitutional infringement on the press and public's right of access to criminal proceedings because the four part inquiry set forth in Cianci was not complied with." (36) The court said, "A better practice would have been to inform prospective jurors carefully in advance that any of them could request to be questioned privately." (37)

In a 1984 case, State v. Cianci (38), the Rhode Island Supreme Court said that presentence reports are confidential and are not to be disclosed to third parties. A presentence report was prepared by a member of the probation department to aid the trial judge in determining an appropriate sentence for the Providence mayor. Information in the report was broadcast by WJAR, Channel 10, and published in articles in *The Providence Journal.* (39) The decision also said that because the Superior Court Rules of Criminal Procedure (40) contain no explicit requirement of confidentiality, nor does the statute that initially authorized presentence reports in felony cases (41), "it would be inappropriate to impose sanctions upon any individual for a violation" of the rule or the law. (42)

The Grand Jury

Proceedings of the grand jury in Rhode Island, unlike most other judicial activities, are closed to the public and the media.

(43) When an indictment is returned, a juror, attorney, interpreter, stenographer, operator of a recording device or a typist who transcribes recorded testimony may disclose matters that occurred before the grand jury only when directed by the court. (44) The court may order an indictment kept secret until the defendant is in custody or has given bail. (45) When an indictment is not returned, disclosure of matters occurring before the grand jury, other than its deliberations or the vote of any juror, may be made only to attorneys for the state in the performance of their duties. (46) When there is no indictment, all notes, transcriptions and recordings of the grand jury proceedings are impounded by the court. (47)

Juveniles and the Courts

Juvenile matters are heard in the Family Court, and Rhode Island law excludes the general public from attending court cases involving children. (48) Only the attorney or attorneys chosen by the parents or guardians of the child and other persons with a direct interest in the case may be present in the courtroom. And all cases involving children must be held separately from the trial of an adult. (49)

This law became the focus of a 1982 case when *The Newport Daily News* asked the state Supreme Court to review an order of a judge of the Family Court barring that newspaper from attending a hearing in a murder case where the defendant was a 14 year old boy because the newspaper had published the name of the youth. The judge also banned reporters from the newspaper from attending future proceedings of the court unless they agreed in advance not to publish the names of the juveniles involved. (50)

The newspaper sought review of the order partly because it said it had obtained the name from nonjudicial sources and had published it — before the hearing began — because the name of the youth was well known in the community. (51) The newspaper argued that if the purpose of the state law (52) was to preserve the anonymity of juvenile offenders appearing before the Family Court by barring the media from the hearings, "the statute failed to accomplish the desired result" in this case. (53) The newspaper also argued that banning its reporters from future hearings was a form of prior restraint (54) and that the "general public" exclusion in the law did not mean the press. (Reporters from *The Providence Journal* who were covering the hearing were not barred because that newspaper did not publish the name.) (55)

Another issue was a 20 year old written agreement that newspapers in the state had with the Family Court. In it the newspapers would be permitted to attend hearings in the court on the understanding that they would not publish the names of the juvenile offenders. (56) However, the Supreme Court attached "no legal significance" to the agreement, adding that "its present existence has not been established." (57)

In its ruling, the state Supreme Court said the Family Court could not penalize the media for publishing lawfully obtained information. (58) It said that the portion of the order conditioning attendance at future court proceedings on agreeing in advance not to publish names was "impermissibly overbroad as well as an unconstitutional prior restraint on the press." (59) The court also ruled that the "general public" clause in the law included the press because it has been established by the U.S. Supreme Court that the Constitution does not "require government to accord the press special access to information not shared by members of the public generally. (60)

The Rhode Island court recommended guidance in dealing with similar cases in the future:

> The media should inform the trial justice of their intentions of making public the name of a juvenile involved in a Family Court proceeding before the proceeding begins. The judge will conduct a hearing at which the media can state for the record "such evidence as the parties deem necessary" con-

cerning the juvenile's identity and the manner in which the information was obtained. If it appears that the media learned the name from judicial sources or that the media learned the name as a result of attendance at a Family Court proceeding, the judge may order the media not to make public the name and may exclude the media from any court proceedings involving that juvenile and possibly other juvenile proceedings. If the source of the name was nonjudicial, the judge may permit the media to make public the name and allow representatives of the media to attend the court proceedings. (61)

Cameras in the Courtroom

In 1981 the Rhode Island Supreme Court adopted Provisional Order No. 15 which permitted the media to film and photograph courtroom proceedings on a one year experimental basis. (62) Previously, cameras were allowed only for non judicial proceedings, such as those involving admission of applicants to the bar or admission of applicants for naturalization. (63)

In 1982, the state's high court extended the experimental period through January 16, 1984. (64) The court chastised the media because "the public understanding of the judicial system and its procedures has not been substantially furthered by television, broadcasting or photographing during the experimental period." (65)

In 1984, the experimental period was again extended for 18 months, with the warning that if the media continued to disregard its "obligation to contribute to public understanding and education during such period" electronic access to the courtrooms would be terminated. (66) The electronic media coverage continued without any formal extension until 1988 when the high court agreed to extend the period indefinitely. However, it will continue to evaluate the effects of cameras in the courtroom. (67) In 1993 with some minor modifications, the provisional order became a permanent part of the Supreme Court's rules. However, a media advisory board of the chief justices of each of the state's courts will continue to evaluate the effects of media access to judicial proceedings. (68)

The electronic media may cover all judicial proceedings in the state's Supreme, Superior, District and Family Courts and those of the Workers' Compensation Commission. No media coverage is permitted in Family Court in respect to juvenile proceedings, adoption proceedings, or other matters in which juveniles are an important part of the proceedings. (69)

A trial justice, "in his or her sole discretion" and with no judicial review available may prohibit cameras in the court-room on the trial justice's own motion or on the request of a participant in the proceeding. (70)

Photographing during the voir dire examination of pro-spective jurors is forbidden, and after the jury is empaneled and sworn in, individual jurors may not be photographed without their consent. Photography is permitted in courtrooms where photographing is impossible without including the jury as part of the background, but closeups that clearly identify individual ju-rors is prohibited. (71) To protect attorney client privilege, there may be no audio pickup or broadcast of conferences which occur in a court facility between the attorney and client, be-tween co counsel of a client, or between counsel and the trial justice held at the bench. (72)

No televising, photographing or broadcasting may take place in courthouse corridors or other parts of the courthouse except in the courtroom during court proceedings and then not during recesses. (73) Such media activity also is forbidden out-side the presence of the jury during or immediately preceding a jury trial. (74)

The presiding justice or judge of the state courts may assign or restrict areas outside a particular courtroom that are used by the media to place equipment and to park vehicles. This may include limitations on the use of land and sidewalks next to the courthouse. If this rule is violated, the judge can exclude those media representatives and/or their equipment from those areas for the duration of the trial or proceeding. (75)

Not more than one television or video tape electronic camera operated by not more than one camera person, is permitted in any trial court. (76) Only one still photographer, using not more than two still cameras with not more than two lenses for each camera and related equipment for print purposes is permitted. (77) Only photographic and audio equipment that does not produce distracting light or sound can be used to cover court proceedings, and television cameras can not use artificial lights. (78) Radio is limited to one audio system. (79) "Pooling" arrangements are made by the media. If a dispute occurs, the trial justice can exclude all media personnel from the trial. (80)

The chief justices of each of the courts in the state can issue special orders concerning the conduct or presence of the media and their equipment outside the courtroom, including areas used for parking vehicles. (81)

Prior Restraint and Contempt of Court

Judges have the power to punish for contempt of court. A civil contempt citation is applied to coerce someone to do something, while a criminal contempt citation is applied to punish disrespect for the court.

In 1986, the Federal District Court in Rhode Island found *The Providence Journal* guilty of criminal contempt for violating a temporary restraining order when it published information about Raymond L.S. Patriarca, the late reputed crime boss in New England. (82) A complex case, it had its roots in 1976 when the *Journal* had requested logs compiled from illegal wiretaps the FBI had conducted at Mr. Patriarca's office in Providence. (83) The FBI refused under the Freedom of Information Act, saying it would be an invasion of Patriarca's privacy to release the logs. (84) The newspaper brought a suit in federal court to compel disclosure. The court held that disclosure of some information, such as details about Mr. Patriarca's private life, could be withheld. (85) The *Journal* appealed. The appeals court said that contents of illegal wiretaps were exempt from disclosure on the ground that it would constitute an invasion of privacy. (86) There the matter remained until Mr. Patriarca died in 1985.

Shortly after that, the *Journal* obtained the logs, but Mr. Patriarca's son, Raymond J. Patriarca, sought a temporary injunction against the newspaper and Channel 10, WJAR television, to halt dissemination of the information in the logs, claiming that his own right to privacy would be invaded. (87) The federal district court entered a temporary restraining order against the newspaper and the television station on Wednesday. The court said it would hear from the newspaper's counsel the next morning on whether the order should be continued. But the *Journal*'s lawyers said they were not prepared to proceed on such short notice, and a hearing was set for Friday.(88) *The Journal,* calling the order "an unconstitutional prior restraint" (89), went ahead and published the contents of some of the logs on Thursday. The newspaper told the court that "to defer publication even for a day was to invite politicians and gangsters to use the same tactics to prevent publication of unfavorable information." (90)

The court found the newspaper and its executive editor, Charles Mc.C. Hauser, guilty of criminal contempt and fined the Journal $100,000 and imposed an 18 month jail term on its editor, which was suspended. Mr. Hauser was ordered to perform 200 hours of public service. The *Journal* appealed the decision. (91) A three judge panel of the U.S. Court of Appeals for the First Circuit ruled that "a transparently invalid court order" could not serve as the basis for a contempt citation. (92) Six months later, the entire panel of judges on the First Circuit issued a second ruling, modifying the earlier ruling. While the court did not reverse its earlier decision voiding the contempt citation against the newspaper, it said that in the future even when a publisher believes his or her newspaper is the subject of a "transparently unconstitutional order of prior restraint," he or she must make "a good faith effort to seek emergency relief" from an appellate court. If timely access to the court is not available or if a timely decision is not forthcoming, the judges said, then the publisher can publish first and then challenge the constitutionality of a restraining order. (93)

At the request of the government prosecutor, the U.S. Supreme Court agreed to review the case. In May, 1988, citing procedural flaws in the government's case, the court let stand the decision of the First Circuit. (94)

If A Court Proceeding Is Closed

Reporters who cover the courts should consider carrying with them the following statement or one similar to it to read to a judge if a motion is made to close the courtroom:

> Your honor, I (your name) am a reporter for (medium). On behalf of my (newspaper/ broadcast outlet), I respectfully would like to object to the motion to close this proceeding to the public, including the press. I request that the court defer its ruling for a brief time to give me the opportunity to contact my (medium) and our legal counsel. Thank you.

Endnotes

1. R.I. Supreme Court Rule 3.6, Trial Publicity.

2. Id.

3. Id.

4. Id.

5. Id. at (a). (In the 1992 murder trial of Raymond D. "Beaver" Tempest in Superior Court, the judge gave the defense lawyer and the prosecutor copies of Supreme Court Rule 3.6 and then asked reporters not to "lead

lawyers into temptation" by asking questions that could have prompted prejudicial responses. (The Providence Journal, March 24, 1992.))

6. Id. at (b).

7. Id. at (b) (1).

8. Id. at (b) (2).

9. Id. at (b) (3).

10. Id. at (b) (4).

11. Id. at (b) (5).

12. Id. at (c) (1).

13. Id. at (c) (2).

14. Id. at (c) (3).

15. Id. at (c) (4).

16. Id. at (c) (5).

17. Id. at (c) (6).

18. Id. at (c) (7) (i).

19. Id. at (c) (7) (ii).

20. Id. at (c) (7) (iii).

21. Id. at (c) (7) (iv).

22. 496 A.2d 139 (RI 1985).

23. Id. at 144.

24. Id., citing Globe Newspaper Co. v. Superior Court, 457 U.S. at 610 11, and 606 607 (1982); Press Enterprise Co. v. Superior Court, 464 U.S. 501 (1984).

25. 496 A. 2d at 144.

26. Id. at 141.

27. Id.

28. Id. at 142.

29. Id.

30. Id.

31. Id. at 145.

32. Id. at 142.

33. The Providence Journal Co. v. Superior Court, 593 A. 2d 446, (RI 1991).

34. Id. at 447.

35. Id.

36. Id. at 449.

37. Id. at 446.

38. 485 A. 2d 565 (RI 1984).

39. Id. at 565.

40. Id. at 567, citing Rule 32.

41. R.I. Gen. Laws 12 19 6.

42. 485 A. 2d at 567.

43. R.I. Superior Court Rules of Criminal Procedure, Rule 6, (2) (e).

44. Id.

45. Id.

46. Id.

47. Id.

48. R.I. Gen. Laws 14 1 30.

49. Id.

50. The Edward A. Sherman Publishing Company v. William R. Goldberg. 443 A. 2d 1252 (RI 1982).

51. Id. at 1256.

52. R.I. Gen. Laws 14 1 30.

53. 443 A. 2d. at 1256.

54. Id.

55. Id. at 1255.

56. Id.

57. Id.

58. Id. at 1257.

59. Id.

60. Id. at 1258, citing Pell v. Procunier, 417 U.S. 817 (1974).

61. Id. at 1259.

62. Section 2 of the Guidelines of Provisional Order No. 15 defines the media as "persons engaged in televising, broadcasting, videotaping and/or photographing (either with still or motion picture camera) of court proceedings." Persons engaged in taking written notes for the printed press are not included in the term "media," except where specifically noted.

63. Supreme Court Rule 30 (B)).

64. In re Extension of Media Coverage for a Further Experimental Period, 454 A 2d 246 (RI 1982).

65. Id. at 247.

66. In re Extension of Media Coverage for a Further Experimental Period 472 A 2d 1233 (RI 1984).

67. In re Permitting of Media Coverage for an Indefinite Period, 539 A 2d 976, (RI 1988).

68. Supreme Court Rules, ARticle VII. Media Coverage of Judicial Proceedings, Canon 13.

69. Id. at Canon 3.

70. Id. at Canon 11.

71. Id. at Canon 10.

72. Id. at Canon 9.

73. Id. at Canon 3 (a).

74. Id. at Canon 3 (b).

75. Id. at Canon 6 (a).

76. Id. at Canon 4 (a).

77. Id. at Canon 4 (b).

78. Id. at Canon 5 (a) (b).

79. Id. at Canon 4 (c).

80. Id. at Canon 4 (d).

81. Id. at Canon 12.

82. Patriarca v. FBI In Re: Providence Journal, 630 F. Supp. 993 (DRI 1986).

83. Providence Journal Co. v. Federal Bureau of Investigation 460 F. Supp. 762 and 778 (DRI 1978).

84. Id. at 763.

85. Id. at 789, 790.

86. The Providence Journal Co. v. Federal Bureau of Investigation 602 F. 2d 1010 (1st Cir. 1979).

87. 630 F. Supp. 993.

88. Id. at 994.

89. Id. at 995.

90. Id.

91. In re Providence Journal, 820 F. 2d 1342, (1st Cir. 1986).

92. Id.

93. In re Providence Journal, 820 F. 2d 1354 (1st Cir. 1987).

94. United States v. Providence Journal, 485 U.S. 693 (1988).

Access to Public Records in Rhode Island

The Rhode Island General Assembly enacted the state's Access to Public Records Act in 1979. (1) The purpose of the law is to "facilitate public access to governmental records which pertain to the policy making functions of public bodies and/or are relevant to the public health, safety, and welfare." (2) At the same time, the legislature intended that the Access to Public Records Act "protect from disclosure information about particular individuals maintained in the files of public bodies when disclosure would constitute an unwarranted invasion of personal privacy." (3) The Rhode Island Supreme Court has said that "it is not required in order to have access to a public document that the purpose of the inquiring party be altruistic and beneficial to the inquiring party." (4)

Defining a Public Body

Public bodies are any executive, legislative, judicial, regulatory, administrative body of the state, or any political subdivision of those bodies. These include departments, divisions, agencies, commissions, boards, offices, bureaus, authorities, school, fire, or water districts, or other state or local agencies which exercise governmental functions. Also public or private agencies, persons, partnerships, corporations or business entities acting on behalf of a public agency are considered public bodies. (5) Judicial bodies are included only in respect to their administrative function. (6)

The public records act states that "public business" means any matter over which the public body has supervision, control, jurisdiction, or advisory power. (7)

Defining Public Records

Public records are all documents, papers, letters, maps, books, tapes, photographs, films, sound recordings, or other material regardless of its physical form or characteristics that is made or received in connection with official business of a state or local public body. (8)

However, the state's attorney general has ruled that this law does not require a city or town to create documents that do not exist at the time of a response to a records request from the public. (9) Nor are public employees required to respond to interview questions (10) or written questions. (11) The law only addresses the accessibility of the records. (12)

Records Specifically Open Under the Law

It is important to note that the following information about public employees is not exempt under the Access to Public Records Act and is open for inspection by the public: the name, gross salary, salary range, total cost of paid fringe benefits, gross amount received in overtime, and other remuneration, in addition to salary, job title, job description, dates of employment and positions held with the state or municipality, work location, business telephone number, the city or town of residence and the date of termination from the job. (13)

Pension records of all persons who are either current or retired members of the retirement system established by the general laws also are open under the act. (14) "Pension records" also include all records concerning retirement credits purchased and the ability of any member of the retirement system to purchase retirement credits. Excluded is information regarding the medical condition of any person and all information identifying the member's designated beneficiaries. (15)

Exemptions to the Act

Personnel and Health Records

The first category of records exempt under the state's Access to Public Records Act deals with all records identifiable to individual applicants for benefits, and to clients, patients, students or employees. (16) These records include, but are not limited to, personnel, medical treatment, welfare, employment security, pupil records, and all records relating to attorney/client relationship and to doctor/patient relationship. (17) In addition, the attorney general has said that individual phone numbers called on cellular phones owned by the city and the locations called from are not public records, but records showing to whom the phones are assigned and the total cost of the phones are public (18)

In addition, records in an individual's file that relate to personal finances, welfare, employment security, student performance, or information in personnel files maintained to hire, evaluate, promote or discipline any employee of a public body are closed. (19)

The state Supreme Court said in 1992 that lists of state employees who were identified for layoff but who werre not laid off, as a result of renegotiation of salaries or of "bumping," are not public records. But lists of employees laid off following complettion of the "bumping" process are public records and are subject to disclosure. (20)

In a similar case, decided three years later, the court ruled that the law does not require public disclosure of the names of teachers who had received nonrenewal notices unless and until the layoffs become final at the end of the school year. The court said non-renewal notices are not final government action and could be rescinded before the end of the school year in light of possible "bumping" of less senior teachers adn the clarification of the school budget. (21)

All personal or medical information relating to an individual in any files, including information relating to medical or psychological facts, is exempt. (22)

A separate state law forbids the release or transferral of a patient's confidential health care information without the written consent of the patient or of his or her authorized representative. The information may be released to other medical personnel or to law officials or the health care provider if they believe a person or his or her family would be in danger from the patient or if the patient is trying to obtain narcotic drugs illegally from the health care provider. (23)

Mental health records may be disclosed only with the written consent of the patient or his or her guardian. (24)

The registration and other records of alcohol treatment facilities are confidential. Information from patients' records may be made public by the state for research purposes, but names and other identifying information cannot be disclosed. (25)

Trade Secrets and Financial Records

The second category of records exempt under the Access to Public Records Act is trade secrets and commercial or financial information obtained from a person, firm, or corporation, that is of a privileged or confidential nature. (26) In 1983 the state Supreme Court interpreted this exemption and the exemption which closes tax returns in Town of New Shoreham v. Rhode Island Public Utilities Commission (27), saying they afforded no right to have made public income tax returns and financial statements which were produced but were sealed in accordance with a protective order by the utilities commission. (28)

In 1990, a nursing center sued the director of the Department of Human Services to prevent disclosure of financial information supplied to the department in compliance with Medicaid requirements. (29) The state's high court rejected the argument stating that, subject to deletion of detailed personnel information which would be identifiable to individual employees and tax returns, the records were public. (30) The court said, "The subjective desire for confidentiality" on the part of the nursing home did not "overcome the public interest in knowing that its tax dollars are being appropriately expended and that its public agencies are properly supervising that expenditure." (31)

Records reflecting the financial settlement by public bodies of any legal claims against a government entity are open. (32)

Child Custody and Adoption Records

Child custody, adoption records, records of illegitimate births, and records of juvenile proceedings before the Family Court are the third category closed under the Access to Public Records Act. (33) Under two separate laws, inspection of the records of an adoption proceeding is prohibited unless disclosure is granted by a court order. (34)

Law Enforcement Records

The fourth exemption deals with all records maintained by law enforcement agencies for criminal law enforcement, and all records relating to the detection and investigation of crime, including those maintained on any individual or compiled in the course of a criminal investigation by any law enforcement agency but only to the extent that the disclosure of such records or information:

(a) could reasonably be expected to interfere with investigations of criminal activity or with enforcement proceedings;

(b) could deprive a person of a right to a fair trial or an impartial adjudication;

(c) could reasonably be expected to constitute an unwarranted invasion of personal privacy;

(d) could reasonably be expected to disclose the identity of a confidential source, including a state, local or foreign agency or authority of any private institution which furnished information on a confidential basis, or the information furnished by such a confidential source;

(e) could disclose techniques and procedures for law enforcement investigations or prosecution, or would disclose guidelines for law enforcement investigations or prosecutions, or

(f) could reasonably be expected to endanger the life or physical safety of an individual. (35)

The exemption states that records specifically open to the public are those relating to the management and direction of a law enforcement agency and those records reflecting the initial arrest of an adult and the charge or charges brought against an adult. (36) This must include the name, address and age, the place of arrest and the name of the arresting officer as well as the charge. (37)

The state's attorney general has said that the law does not require police departments to provide oral information to the public concerning arrests. (38)

A separate law prohibits public access to information contained in emergency 911 telephone calls. (39)

The Rhode Island Supreme Court first interpreted the Access to Public Records Act in The Rake v. Gorodetsky (40) in 1982 when it ruled police records of civilian complaints of police brutality were not exempt from disclosure since the reports were not considered personnel records simply because the police department regarded them as such. (41) The court noted that the reports did not identify the citizen complainants or the police officers because the names of both were deleted. (42)

Records not Available to Litigants

Exemption five denies access to any records which would not be available by law or rule of court to an opposing party in litigation. (43) In Hydron Labs, Inc. v. Department of the Attorney General, the state Supreme Court said that where documents were determined to be the work product of the attorney general and thus privileged, in a criminal action charging the laboratory with environmental violations, those documents were exempt from disclosure. (44) The court said that it was never the General Assembly's intent to give litigants a greater right of access to documents through the state's open records law than those litigants would have under the Superior Court Rules of Civil Procedure that provide for litigation discovery and place appropriate limits on the scope of that discovery. (45)

Other Exemptions Under the Act

Scientific and technological secrets and the security plans of military and law enforcement agencies are not open to the public when disclosure would endanger the public welfare and security. (46)

Any records which disclose the identity of the contributor of a bona fide and lawful charitable contribution to the public body whenever public anonymity has been requested are unavailable for public inspection. (47)

Reports and statements of strategy or negotiation involving labor negotiations or collective bargaining are closed, (38) as are reports and statements of strategy or negotiation with respect to the investment or borrowing of public funds, until such time as those transactions are entered into. (49)

Not open to public inspection are any minutes of a meeting of a public body which are not required to be disclosed under the state's Open Meetings Law. (50) Preliminary drafts, notes, impressions, memoranda, working papers and work products of state and local public bodies are closed. (51) Also closed

97

are correspondence of or to elected officials with or relating to those they represent, and correspondence of or to elected officials in their official capacities. (52)

Test questions, scoring keys and other examination data used to administer a licensing examination, an examination for employment or promotion, or academic examinations are closed, provided that a person has the right to review the results of his or her examination. (53) Also closed are records of individual test scores on professional certification and licensing examinations, provided that the person has the right to review his or her examination results. (54)

Not open for public inspection are the contents of real estate appraisals, engineering or feasibility estimates and evaluations made for or by an agency relative to the acquisition of property or to prospective public supply and construction contracts, until such time as all property has been acquired or all proceedings or transactions have been terminated or abandoned, provided that the law of public domain is not affected by this provision. (55)

All tax records are closed under the Access to Public Records Act. (56)

Closed are all investigatory records of public bodies pertaining to possible violations of statute, rule, or regulation other than records of final actions taken, provided that all records prior to formal notification of violations and noncompliance are not be deemed to be public. (57) Requests for advisory opinions are closed until such time as the public body issues its opinions. (58)

Records, reports, opinions, information, and statements required to be kept confidential by federal or state law, rule, rule of court, or regulation or state statute are closed. (59)

Library records which, by themselves, or when examined with other public records, would reveal the identity of the library user requesting, checking out or using any library materials are not open for public inspection. (60) Also closed are printouts from telecommunication devices for the deaf or hearing and speech impaired. (61)

Personal information in an individual's motor vehicle record is not open to the general public, although it can be disclosed for law enforcement and judicial purposes, for motor vehicle safety, for bulk marketing purposes and some other narrowly tailored uses. (62)

Commission on Judicial Tenure and Discipline

The transcript and the findings, conclusions and recommendation of the commission regarding the reprimand, suspension, censure, removal or retirement of a member of the judiciary are public documents. The exception is when the documents relate to a hearing concerning a private reprimand. These are confidential records. (63) In addition, all papers filed with, proceedings before and decisions of the state Supreme Court on review of such reprimands are closed. (64) Evidence obtained by the commission is confidential until it is introduced or becomes the subject of testimony at a public hearing. (65) Papers filed in judicial proceedings in aid of or ancillary to a non public commission hearing are confidential. (66) The provisions in this chapter are expressly exempt from the operation of the Access to Public Records Act. (67)

Other Statutory Exemptions

Child custody records are confidential but may be disclosed, when necessary, to certain health care officials, to the Family Court, and to the attorney general's department. They also may be disclosed to inform a person who has made a report of child abuse or neglect whether services have been provided to the child as a result of the report. (68) All court records which concern the identity of a victim of child molestation sexual assault are confidential (69), although a defendant charged with the crime may apply to the court for an order of disclosure of identifying information to prepare a defense. The defendant may give the information to his or her lawyer and others involved directly in the preparation of the defense. Any other disclosure constitutes contempt. (70)

Welfare records are closed to public inspection, although they may be subpoenaed for litigation directly connected with the administration of public assistance. (71) Registration and other records of alcohol treatment facilities are closed. (72) Records regarding to the ownership of or security interests in registered public obligations are closed. (73)

Vital Statistics

Disclosure of birth, death and marriage records is not allowed (74) unless the state's director of health approves for research purposes. (75) Records of births out of wedlock can not be disclosed without a court order. (76) Records of persons born 100 years or more ago can be approved for genealogical research. (77)

Procedural Matters

Right To Inspect and Copy Records

Except for those records specifically closed by law, all records maintained or kept on file by any public body, whether or not required by any law, rule or regulation, are public records and every person shall have the right to inspect and/or copy the records at a reasonable time to be determined by the custodian of the materials. (78) The public body must make, keep and maintain written or recorded minutes of all meetings. (79) And each one shall establish procedures regarding access to the records. (80) If the public record is in active use or in storage and therefore not available when a person requests access, the custodian of the records must inform the person and make an appointment for him or her to inspect the records "as expeditiously as they may be made available." (81) Any public body which maintains its records in a computer storage system shall provide a printout of any data properly identified. (82) However, the public body need not reorganize, consolidate, or compile data not maintained in the form requested at the time the request to inspect the records was made. (83)

Cost

The cost of written documents shall not exceed 15 cents a page for those copyable on business or legal size paper. (84) A reasonable charge may be made for the search or retrieval of documents. Costs shall not exceed $15 an hour, and no charge shall be made for the first 30 minutes of search or retrieval. (785) Copies of documents shall be provided and the search and retrieval of documents accomplished within a reasonable time after a request. The public body shall provide an estimate of the costs prior to providing the copies. (86)

Denial of Access and Administrative Appeals

Any denial of access to public records shall be made to the person requesting them by the public official who has custody or control of the records in writing giving the specific reasons for the denial within 10 business days of the request, and indicating the procedures for appealing the denial. (87) Failure to comply with a request to inspect or copy public records within the 10 day period shall be considered a denial. This limit may be extended for a period not to exceed 30 days. (88)

A person denied the right to inspect a record of a public body by the custodian of the record may petition the chief administrative officer of that public body for a review of the denial. The officer must make a final determination on whether to allow public inspection within 10 business days after submission of the review petition. (789) If the officer determines that the record is closed to the public, the person seeking the disclosure may file a complaint with the attorney general, who then shall investigate the complaint. If he or she determines the complaint has merit, he or she may institute proceedings for injunctive or declaratory relief on behalf of the complainant in the Superior Court in the county where the record is kept. A complainant also may retain private counsel to institute court proceedings. (90)

The Superior Court may examine any record which is the subject of a suit in the privacy of his or her chambers to determine whether the record or any part of it may be withheld from public inspection under the terms of the Access to Public Records Act. (91) The court may fine a public body or public official found to have violated the act up to $1,000. (92)

The Access to Public Records Act states that in all actions brought under the act, the burden is on the public body to demonstrate that the record in dispute may be properly withheld from public inspection. (93) In 1991, the Rhode Island Supreme Court ruled that the Access to Public Records Act does not provide an injunctive remedy to persons or entities seeking to block disclosure of records; it only provides a remedy for those denied access to public records. (94) A local of a teachers union had sought an injunction against disclosure by the governor of the state of records relating to special pension benefits authorized by the legislature for the state retirement system. (95)

The Access to Public Records Act may not be construed as preventing a public body from opening its records concerning its administration to public inspection. (96)

Commercial Use of Public Records

No person or business may use information obtained from public records to solicit for commercial purposes, or to obtain a commercial advantage over the party furnishing that information to a public body. Anyone who knowingly does so shall, in addition to any civil liability, be fined up to $500 and/or be imprisoned for up to one year. (97)

Endnotes

1. RI. Gen. Laws 382-I et seq. Prior to 1979, common law allowed a person access to public records only if he or she required such records "to maintain or defend an action for which the document or record sought" could supply the necessary information. Daluz v. Hawksley, 351 A.2d 820 (R.L 1976).

2. 38-2-1.

3. Id. A separate law, 28-6.4-1, permits an employee to inspect his or her personnel files in the workplace in the presence of an employer or an employer's designee. Files may not be removed by the employee nor may he or she make copies. In Providence Journal Co. v. Sundlun, the state supreme court ruled that while the underlying policy of the law favors the free flow and disclosure of information to the public, "the legislature did not intend to empower the press and the public with carte blanche to demand all records held by public agencies" 616 A2d 1132 CR.!. 1992)

4. Charlesgate Nursing Center v. Bordeleau, 568 A.2d 775 (RI. 1990).

5. 38-2-2 (2).

6. 38-2-2 (d) (20).

7. 38-2-2 (b).

8. Id. at (d).

9. Op. Atty. Gen PR96-02, P1(96-10, PR97-07, P1(97-14 and PR97-23.

10. Op. Atty. Gen. P1(95-20.

11. Op. Atty. Gen. PR96-17.

12. Op. Any. Gen. PR9S-20.

13. 38-2-2 (d) (1). An individual employee's number is not public information and providing It would constitute an unwarranted invasion of privacy. Op. Atty. Gen. PR95-13. In 1991 the General Assembly revised the Access to Public Records Act after the Rhode Island Supreme Court in 1990 upheld a decision by the state to deny The Providence journal access to certain records relating to state employees Providence Journal Co. v. Kane, 577 A.2d 661.

14. 3&2-2 (d) (1).

15. Id.

16. Id.

17. Id.

18. Op. Atty. Gen. PR95-30 and 31.

19. 38-2-2- (d) (1). Dates, locations and titles of courses taken by individual state employees under the incentive In-service training programs are not public. AG

OpPR96-07. But records of funds paid by a town for law school tuition and related expenses of the police chief are public record. AG Op PR96-12.

20. Providence Journal Co. v. Sundlun, 616 A.2d 1131 (RI. 1992). The court said that no public interest is served by disclosing the names of employees who have not been laid off from state employment. Any state employee named in a potential layoff list is entitled to his or her privacy until such time as final action is taken which results from separation from state employment. Id. at 1136. In Pawtucket Teachers Alliance Local No. 920, AFT, AFL-CIO, v. Brady, 556 A.2d 556 (R.l. 1989), said that a management study of an elementary school operation, relating specifically to the job performance of the principal, was exempt from public disclosure because it came within the personnel record exception. (18)

21. Edward A. Sherman Publishing Co. and The Providence Journal Co. v. E. Richard Carpender, 659 A.2d 1117 (Ri. 1995).

22. RI. General Laws 38-2-(d) (1). The law does not require disclosure to an inmater of all his psychology reports, periodic reports, evaluations and conclusions associated with the parole section of his file. AG Op 95-19

23. R.I. Gen. Laws 5-37.3-4.

24. R.l. Gen. Laws 40.1-5-26.

25. 40.1-4-13 (1) (2).

26. 38-2-2 (d) (2). The computer field description from a city's computerized financial data bases are not public record because it is part of a program licensed from a private company, but the column headings as they appear on the computer screen or on a hardcopy print are public record. AG Op PR96-14 and 14A.

27. 464 A.2d 730.

28. Id.

29. 568 A.2d at 775.

30. Id.

31. Id. at 777.

32. R.t. General Laws 38-2-14.

33. 38-2-2 (d) (3). The Ri. Supreme Court said the victim of a juvenile crime who sues the offender can have access to the juvenile's police records

for purposes of the civil litigation, if the Family Court determines there is good cause for releasing the records. Falstaff Brewing Corp. in Re: Narragansett Brewery Fire, 637 A.2d 1047 (R.I. 1994).

34. RI. Gen. Laws 8-10-21, and 23-3-15. In it Christine, 397 A.2d 511 (R.I. 1979), a natural mother sought access to records of the adoptive parents, and In re Assalone, 512 A.2d 1383 (RI. 1985), an adult adoptee brought action to gain access to records identifying her biological parents. In both cases, the Rhode Island Supreme Court found insufficient cause for disclosure.

35. 38-2-2 (d) (4). Records of the Adult Correctional Institution which are maintained for the purposes of enforcing criminal laws or to investigate possible violations of laws, rules or regulations are not public records. AG Op PR95-19.

36. Id.

37. Op. Arty. Gen. PR95-O1 and PR95-07.

38. Op. Arty. Gen. PR95-07.

39. 39-21.1-4. Police department policy that pertains to response codes and dispatcher assignments is not considered public information. Op. Atty. Gen. PR97-12.

40. 452 A.2d 1144.

41. Id.

42. Id.

43. 38.2-2 (d) (5).

44. 492 A.2d 135 (R.l. 1985).

45. Id. at 139.

46. 38-2-2 (d) (6).

47. Id. at (7).

48. Id. at (8).

49. Id. at (9).

50. Id. at (10).

51. Id. at (11).

52. Id. at (13).

53. Id. at (12).

54. Id. at (17).

55. Id. at (14).

56. Id. at (15).

57. Id. at (16).

58. Id. at (18). 5

9. Id. at (19).

60. Id. at (21).

61. Id. at (22).

62. R.I. Gen. Laws 27-49-3.1.

63. RI. Gen. Laws 8-16.5.

64. R.I. Gen. Laws 8-16-7.1.

65. RI. Gen. Laws 8-16-13.

66. RI. Gen. Laws 8-16-13.1.

67. RI. Gen. Laws 38-2-2(d) (20).

68.111. Gen. Laws 42-72-8.

69. R.I. Gen. Laws 11-37.8.5 (a).

70. Id. at (c).

71. Ri. Gen. Laws 40-6-12.

72. R.I. Gen. Laws 40-1413 (1).

73. Ri. Gen. Law 35-13-11 (a).

74. RI. Gen. Laws 23-3-23.

75. Id. at (a) (b).

76. Id. at (c).

77. Id. at (d).

78. R.I. Gen. Laws 38-2.3 (a).

79. Id. at (b).

80. Id. at (c).

81. Id. at (d).

82. Id. at (e).

83. Id. at (f).

84. R.I. Gen. Laws 38-2-4 (a).

85. Id. at (b).

86. Id. at (c). The law does not require a public body to provide an itemization for each document retrieval and legal support for each charge associated with the retrieval. AG Op PR96-16.

87. R.I. Gen. Laws 38-2-7 (a).

88. Id. at (b).

89. R.I. Gen. Laws 38-2-8 (a).

90. Id. at (b).

91. R.I. Gen. Laws 38-9-2(b).

92. Id. at (c).

93. R.I. Gen. Laws 38-2-10.

94. RI. Federation of Teachers, AFT, AFL-CIO v. Sundlun, 595 A.2d 799 (R.1. 1991).

95. Id. The slate court cited Chrysler Corp. v. Brown, 99 S.Ct 1705 (1979) in which the Court of Appeals for the Third Circuit held that the federal Freedom of Information Act was exclusively a disclosure statute and provided no remedy for one who sought to compel nondisclosure.

96. III. Gen. Laws 38-2-5(a).

97. R.I. Gen. Laws 38-2-6.

Open Meetings in Rhode Island

The state's Open Meetings Law was enacted in 1976 to ensure that public business would "be performed in an open and public manner" and to allow citizens to "be advised of and aware of the performance of public officials and the deliberations and decisions that go into the making of public policy." (1)

Every meeting of all municipal and state public bodies in Rhode Island must be open to the public except when certain matters, specified in the Open Meetings Law, are being discussed. (2) Financial town meetings are open to all, with no distinction between registered and non registered voters. (3) The law does not prohibit sound and photographic recordings, although the use of electronic communication may not be used "to circumvent the spirit or the requirements" of the law. (4) The law does allow for the removal of a person who "willfully disrupts a meeting to the extent that orderly conduct of the meeting is seriously compromised." (5)

Defining a Public Body

Covered under the law is any department, agency, commission, committee, board, council, bureau, or authority of any subdivision of state or local government. A political party or organization meeting for any purpose is not considered a public body. (6)

The law does not apply to proceedings of the judicial branch of government, and probate and municipal court proceedings in any city or town. (7)

A meeting is defined by law as the convening of a public body to discuss and/or act upon a matter over which the public body has supervision, control, jurisdiction or advisory power. A meeting also refers to so called "workshop," "working" or "work" sessions. (8) A memorandum from a mayor circulated among council members requesting that plans for a landfill be kept secret does not constitute a meeting under the Open Meetings Law, but the state's attorney general has ruled that the memorandum "implicitly endorses the circumvention" of the law and such conduct "will not be condoned." (9) Members of a public body conducting telephone meetings are in violation of the law. (10) And a superintendent discussing business with two members of the school committee in her office may be considered a meeting under the law. (11)

A quorum means a simple majority of the membership of the public body. (12) The attorney general has ruled that newly elected but not officially installed members of a city council are subject to the law. (13)

Public Notice Requirement

By law, public bodies must give written notice of their regularly scheduled meetings at the beginning of each calendar year. The notice must include the dates, times, and places of the meetings. (14) In addition, public bodies must give written public notice of any meeting within at least 48 hours before the date. Included must be the date, time, place, and a statement specifying the nature of the business to be discussed. However, public bodies, with the exception of school committees, are free to add items to the agenda by a majority vote of the members. (15) Continuations of public meetings must receive the same degree of advance notice as the original meeting. (16)

Written public notice must be posted at the principal office of the public body holding the meeting, and if no such office exists, the notice must be posted at the building in which the meeting is to be held, as well as at one other prominent place in a government unit. School committee notices also must be published in a newspaper of general circulation in the school district under the committee's jurisdiction. A public body can hold an emergency meeting, if a majority of its members agree, when the meeting is deemed necessary because the public welfare requires it. If an emergency meeting is called, written notice and an agenda must be posted as soon as practicable.(17)

Closed Meetings

A public body may hold a closed meeting by an "open call" upon an affirmative vote of a majority of its members. (18) A meeting closed to the public must be limited to matters allowed to be exempted by law. (19) The vote of each member, the reason for holding the closed meeting, and a statement specifying the nature of the business to be discussed must be recorded and entered into the minutes of the meeting. (20)

A public body may hold a meeting closed to the public for one or more of the following purposes: (21)

- Discussions of the job performance, character, or physical or mental health of a person or persons, provided that the person or persons affected may require that the discussion be held at an open meeting. (22)
- Sessions or work sessions pertaining to collective bargaining or litigation. (23)
- Discussions of security matters, including but not limited to the deployment of security personnel or devices. (24)
- Investigative proceedings regarding allegations of misconduct, either civil or criminal. (25)
- Discussions or considerations related to the acquisition or lease of real property for public purposes, of the disposition of publicly held property where advance public information would be detrimental to the public interest. (26)

- Discussions concerning a prospective business or industry locating in the state when an open meeting would have a detrimental effect on the public interest. (27)
- A matter related to the question of public funds where the premature disclosure would adversely affect the public interest. Public funds include any investment plan or matter related thereto, including but not limited to state lottery plans for new promotions. (28)
- Any executive sessions of a local school committee exclusively for the purposes of (a) conducting student disciplinary hearings, or (b) of reviewing other matters which relate to the privacy of students and their records, unless the student asks for the discussion to be held in public. (29)

The attorney general has said that school committees may lawfully close meetings to conduct "self evaluation" sessions. (30) But "gripe sessions" by a city council to hear complaints from the community about the council are public meetings under the Open Meetings Law, and minutes are required. (31)

Minutes

All public bodies must keep written minutes of their meetings. (32) The minutes should include:

- The date, time, and place of the meeting. (33)
- The members of the public body recorded as either present or absent. (34)
- A record by individual members of any vote taken. (35)
- Any other information relevant to the business of the public body that any member asks to be included or reflected in the minutes. (36)

A record of all votes taken at all meetings of public bodies, listing how each member voted on each issue, becomes a public record and must be made available at the office of the public body within two weeks of the date of the vote. Unofficial minutes must be available at the office within 35 days of

the meeting or at the next regularly scheduled meeting, whichever is earlier. Exceptions are where the public body has voted
to close the minutes of an executive session or where by a
majority vote it extends the time period for filing the minutes
and publicly states the reason. (37)

The minutes of a closed session shall be made available
at the next regularly scheduled meeting unless a majority of the
public body votes to keep the minutes closed. (38)

Public bodies in the executive branch of the state government must file with the secretary of state copies of all records
of votes and all minutes of meetings within one week of the
date of their availability. Excluded are public bodies whose re-
sponsibilities are only advisory. (39)

Violations

Filing a Complaint

If an individual believes that a meeting of a public body
has violated any portion of the Open Meetings Law, that person can file a complaint with the attorney general, who then
must investigate. If the attorney general determines the complaint has merit, he or she may file a complaint against the
public body on behalf of the citizen in the Superior Court. (40)

The complaint must be filed within 90 days from the date
of public approval of the minutes of the meeting at which the
alleged violation occurred, or in the case of an unannounced or
improperly closed meeting within 90 days of the public action
of a public body revealing the alleged violation, whichever is
greater. (41)

If a person files a complaint with the attorney general,
and the attorney general fails to take legal action, that person
can retain private counsel and file suit in Superior Court within
90 days of the attorney general's closing of the complaint or
within 180 days of the alleged violation, whichever comes first.
(42)

Fines Against Public Bodies

The Superior Court can issue injunctive relief and declare null and void any action of a public body found to be in violation of the Open Meetings Law. In addition, the court can fine the public body or any of its members up to $5,000 and may award reasonable attorney fees and costs to the prevailing plaintiff. (43)

When the attorney general determines there has been a violation of the law, the usual practice has been to send the public body a non-binding, written opinion informing it that it has violated the law or to ask the public body to reconvene in public and take a new vote. Some of the more recent opinions are incorporated into the appropriate endnotes for this chapter.

Notice of Citizen Rights

The attorney general must prepare a notice providing concise information explaining the requirements of the Open Meetings Law and advising citizens of their right to file complaints for violations of the law. The notice must be posted in a prominent location in every city and town hall in the state. (44)

Summary of Complaints and Actions

Each year the attorney general must prepare for the General Assembly a report summarizing the complaints. The summary must include information as to how many complaints were found to be meritorious and the action taken by the attorney general in response to the complaints. (45)

Endnotes

1. RI. Gen. Laws 42.46-1.

2. RI. Gen. Laws 42-46-3. A letter discussing agenda items scheduled for a public meeting does not constitute a meeting, but the attorney general's office "seeks to discourage individual public officers from attempting to conduct public business via the mail" (Op. Atty. Gen. No. U91/45, Nov. 20, 1991). In 1995, the Superior Court ruled that a financial town meeting does

not fall within the definition of a public body and therefore does not meet the provisions of the law. (The Providence Journal-Bulletin, July 9.)

3. RI. Gen. Laws 42-46-5(b). In Belcherv. Mansi, 569 F. Supp. 379 (DRI 1983), the federal district court ruled that a community school committee must allow the tape recording of its public (nonexecutive, nonexempt) sessions.

4. Id. at (d).

5. Op. Atty. Gen. 0M97-12.

6. R.I. Gen. Laws 42.46-2(c). A senatorial district committee is not a unit of state or municipal government, so is not a public body under the law (Op. Atty. Gen. OM96-24). The East Greenwich Fire District Apparatus Committee is a committee of municipal government and must comply with the law (Op. Airy. Gen. 0M96-36).

7. R.I. Gen. Laws 42-46-5 (c). Four individuals from different state and city agencies and departments who meet are not considered a public body under the law (Op. Any. Gen. 0M95-14).

8. R.I. Gen. Laws 42.46-2(a). In 1996, the R.I. Supreme Court said that although members of a school committee and a superintendent held a meeting without the newspaper notification listing an agenda for a "work session," they did not act willfully or in bad faith since they did not attempt to keep the meeting or its agenda a secret. Their action at the meeting should not be declared null and void (Edwards v. State, 677 A.2d 1347). A meeting between a mayor and a town solicitor does not constitute a meeting under the law (Op. Arty. Gen. No. U92/26, March 19, 1992). A meeting of members of a fire district to pay bills is a meeting and is subject to the law (Op. Arty. Gen. 0M97-08).

9. Op. Atty. Gen. No. 1.192/17, Feb. 27, 1992.

10. Op. Arty. Gen. Unnumbered, Dec. 4, 1989.

11. Op. Atty. Gen. 0M96-34.

12. RI. Gen. Laws 42-46-2 (c).

13. Op. Atty. Gen. 0M95-31.

14. RI. Gen. Laws 42.46.6(a). In 1997. the Superior Court fined three members of the High School Building Commmlttee, an advisory committee to the Barrington School Committee, for violating the open meetings law by participating in four unadvertised, unposted meetings of the the advisory committee. (The Providence Journal-Bulletin, April 18.)

15. Id. at (b). There Is no requirement under the law that public bodies provide notice of the specific time that a particular agenda item will be addressed at the meeting (Op. Atty. Gen. OM97-10).

16. Op. Atty. Oat. No. 91/8/14, Aug. 14, 1991.

17. 42.46.6 at (c).

18. RI. Gen. Laws 42.46-4. The public body is not required to hold a closed session after the completion of a meeting as long as it convenes the open meeting first and notes in the open meeting it will convene in closed session (Op. Any. Gen. 0M95-20).

19. Id. The specific subsection of the law and the nature of the business to be discussed must be announced before convening in closed session. Moving to convene "under appropriate rule" does not meet the requirements of the law (Op. Atty. Gen. 0M97-11.)

20. Id. In R.I. Affiliate, American Civil Liberties Union v. Bernasconi, 557 A.2d 1232, (R.I. 1989), the state Supreme Court held that a school committee's closedsession discussion and approval of a drug search of student lockers was a matter exempt from the requirements of the Open Meetings Law. The ACLU held that the school committee failed to cite accurately the correct exception to the law, an argument the court said lacked merit. The ACLU also argued that the drug search issue was not listed on the posted agenda, but the court said that an announcement of the subject matter before the meeting would have been self-defeating.

21. R.I. Gen. Laws 42-46-5.

22. Id. at (1). The attorney general has ruled that interviews with job applicants must be public, but deliberations on character and job pcformance may be closed (Op. Atty. Oat. No. 89/3/19, March 17, 1989). Nothing in the Open Meetings Law 'authorizes completely secretive interviews of (Job) candidates" (Op. Atty. Gen. No. 89/4/24, April 10, 1989).

23. Id. at (2). This exemption can be used for imminent legal proceedings as well as actual ones (Op. Atty. Gen. No. 88/3/18, March 21, 3988). It also covers "collective bargaining" with a group of Individuals treated similarly in a contractual context. It is not necessary to have a formally recognized and/or certified collective bargaining unit for a public body to engage in collective bargaining under the law (Op. Atty. Gen. 0M96-19.)

24. Id. at 0).

25. Id. at (4).

26. Id. at (5).

27. Id. at (6).

28. Id. at (7).

29. Id. at (8).

30. Op. Atty. Gen. No. 90/4/13, April 28, 1990.

31. Op. Any. Gen. No. 90/12/41, Dec. 4, 1990.

32. RI. Gen. Laws 42-46.7 (a).

33. RI. Gen. Laws 42-467 (a) (1).

34. Id. at (2).

35. Id. at (3).

36. Id. at (4).

37. R.L Gen. Laws 42-467 (b).

38. Id. at (c).

39. Id.at(d).

40. RI. Gen. Laws 42-468 (a).

41. Id. at (b).

42. Id. at (c).

43. Id. at (d).

44. RI. Gen. Laws 42-46-12.

45. RI. Gen. Laws 42-46.11.

1772342

Made in the USA